**ATTENTION READER:**
PLEASE NOTE THAT THIS IS
NOT A FINISHED BOOK.

A bound galley is the first stage of printer's proofs, which has not been corrected by the author, publisher, or printer.

The design, artwork, page length, and format are subject to change, and typographical errors will be corrected during the course of production.

If you quote from this galley, please indicate that your review is based on uncorrected text.

Thank you,
Viking

# THE BOYS IN THE BOAT

DANIEL JAMES BROWN

978-0-451-47592-3
Ages: 10 up / Grades: 5 up
Pages: 240
Trim: 7" x 9"
Territory: E00
Price: U.S. $17.99 / CAN. $20.99
Also available on audio from Listening Library:
US $35.00 (CAN $42.00): CD ISBN 978-1-101-92585-0 /
Audio download ISBN: 978-1-101-92586-7

**Daniel James Brown** is the author of the #1 *New York Times* bestseller *The Boys in the Boat*, which won the ABA Nonfiction Book of the Year Award and the Washington State Book Award. His two previous nonfiction books, *The Indifferent Stars Above* and *Under a Flaming Sky*, were both finalists for the Washington State Book Award. He has taught writing at San Jose State University and Stanford University. He lives outside Seattle.

You can learn more at danieljamesbrown.com.

A beloved story about beating the odds and finding hope in the most desperate times, newly adapted for young readers

OUT OF THE DEPTHS of the Great Depression comes the astonishing tale of nine working-class boys from the American West who at the 1936 Olympics showed the world what true grit really meant. With rowers who were the sons of loggers, shipyard workers, and farmers, the University of Washington's eight-oar crew was never expected to defeat the elite East Coast teams, yet they did, going on to shock the world by challenging the German boat rowing for Adolf Hitler.

At the center of the tale is Joe Rantz, a teenager without family or prospects, whose personal quest captures the spirit of his generation— the generation that would prove in the coming years that the Nazis could not prevail over American determination and optimism.

This deeply emotional yet easily accessible young readers adaptation of the award-winning #1 *New York Times* bestseller features never-before-seen photographs, highly visual back matter, and an exclusive new introduction.

# THE
# BOYS
## IN THE
# BOAT

The True Story of an American Team's Epic Journey
to Win Gold at the 1936 Olympics

# DANIEL JAMES BROWN
## Adapted for young readers by GREGORY MONE

## VIKING
An Imprint of Penguin Group (USA)

VIKING
Published by the Penguin Group
Penguin Group (USA) LLC
375 Hudson Street
New York, New York 10014

USA * Canada * UK * Ireland * Australia
New Zealand * India * South Africa * China

penguin.com
A Penguin Random House Company

First published in the United States of America by Viking, an imprint of Penguin Young Readers Group, 2015
This work is based on *The Boys in the Boat: Nine Americans and Their Epic Quest for Gold at the 1936 Berlin Olympics*, by Daniel James Brown, copyright © 2013 by Blue Bear Endeavors, LLC, published by Viking, an imprint of Penguin Group (USA) Inc.

Copyright © 2015 by Blue Bear Endeavors, LLC

LIBRARY OF CONGRESS CATALOGING-IN-PUBLICATION DATA IS AVAILABLE
ISBN: 978-0-451-47592-3

Manufactured in China

10  9  8  7  6  5  4  3  2  1

Designed by Jim Hoover

dedication TK

# WHO'S WHO

## FAMILY

**Joe Rantz:** Abandoned throughout his childhood, he quit trusting people until he found rowing, which forced him to put his faith in his crew.

**Harry Rantz:** A mechanic and inventor who left his son Joe to live on his own, then reconciled with him later in life.

**Thula Rantz:** Harry's second wife, and stepmother to Joe, she once had hopes of becoming a famous musician.

**Joyce Simdars:** The teenage girl who sang along with Joe in the back of their school bus became the joy of his life and, eventually, his wife.

## THE BOAT

**Roger Morris, Bow:** Quiet, strong Roger Morris was one of Joe's first friends at the University of Washington.

**Chuck Day, Seat Two:** A quick-tempered prankster built of pure muscle, he worked with Joe at the Grand Coulee dam.

**Gordy Adam, Seat Three:** A former salmon fisherman who grew up on a dairy farm, he earned the nickname "Courage" because he rowed one race with his thumb cut to the bone.

**Johnny White, Seat Four:** Shorter than Joe, but thin and strong, he graduated high school two years early. In the summer of '35, he toiled at the Grand Coulee dam with Joe and Chuck.

**Jim "Stub" McMillin, Seat Five:** A six-foot-five beanpole who never gave up on a race, he worked his way through college, just like Joe.

**George "Shorty" Hunt, Seat Six:** The chatty former high school sports star would eventually be named one of Washington's greatest oarsmen.

**Joe Rantz, Seat Seven:** Although he'd never rowed before college, the years he spent logging, digging ditches, and building roads built the muscles that made him a powerful force in the boat.

**Don Hume, Stroke:** A curly-haired kid who never showed pain, he was nearly too sick to stand before the Olympics, but he still stroked the boys to victory.

**Bobby Moch, Coxswain:** The brains and strategic genius of the boat, he helped the crew find its swing in a series of come-from-behind victories.

## COACHES

**Al Ulbrickson:** A well-dressed former champion oarsman himself, the varsity coach achieved his lifelong dream when the boys took gold in Berlin.

**George Pocock:** The British boatbuilder designed and built the boys their winning shell, but he also gave Joe and the coaches valuable advice about the nature of the sport.

# CONTENTS

# A NOTE FROM THE AUTHOR

Ever since *The Boys in the Boat* was first published, I have been traveling around the country talking to people about the story. When I first started, I quickly noticed that most of the people in my audiences were quite old. Some of them, in fact, were old enough to remember the events at the heart of the story, even though those events took place almost eighty years ago.

But lately something interesting has begun to happen. More and more young people have begun to show up at my book talks. Often these younger people join with the older people, coming up to the front of the room to have their book signed. Frequently they pause at the signing table just to tell me how much they enjoyed the story and what it means to them personally. It sometimes seems strange to me to have a ninety-year-old grandma and a twelve-year-old student standing next to each other in front of me at the signing table. But listening to what both groups of readers have to say about the story I have begun to understand. Some things are timeless.

At first glance, this may seem to be a story about a time and place that is very different from the time and place you live in. After all, the young men at the center of this story dressed very differently than you and your friends do. They talked differently. They drove cars that look now as if they belong in museums. They sang songs that sound corny to our modern ears. They thought a radio was a marvel of modern technology. They lived through world events that now seem almost like ancient history.

But here's the thing. The boys in the boat were just that, boys. The problems they wrestled with were the same that you and your friends likely wrestle with today: family problems, making the team, succeeding at school, fitting in with other kids, learning whom you can and can't trust, finding a way to make some money, figuring out how you feel about the opposite sex, deciding who and what you want to be a few years down the road. Under the surface, they really weren't all that different.

None of that, though, is really what the young people who come up to me at book events want to talk about. What they recognize in the story—and what they want to share with me—is the sheer excitement of being young, having a goal, striving to accomplish that goal, and making it happen, just as the boys in the boat did. Sometimes they talk about their volleyball team winning the regionals. Sometimes they talk about making first violin in the school orchestra. Sometimes they talk about wanting to be the first in their family to go to college. Sometimes they talk about falling short of their goal but being inspired by the book to try again.

It is easy for those of us who are older and count ourselves wise to forget that it is the young who most often move the world forward. It is the young who have the boundless energy, passion, optimism, courage, and idealism to try to do what we elders might say is impossible. That's what the boys in the boat attempted to do in this story. That's why, eighty years later at my book-signing table, old men and women come to me with tears in their eyes, proudly remembering when they were young and full of fire. And it's why standing right next to them are young men and women with beaming faces, bearing tales of their own brave attempts at the near impossible.

So as you read this book, I hope that you will keep in mind that at its heart this is a story about growing up, about wresting with hope and doubt, about dreaming big, about going for the gold. In that sense, it's really a story about you.

Dawn row on Lake Washington.

# Prologue

This book is a true story. It was born on a cold, drizzly, late spring day, several years ago, when I climbed over a split-rail cedar fence and made my way to the modest house where Joe Rantz lay dying.

Joe was my neighbor Judy's father, and she had asked me to come down and meet him. I knew only two things about him when I knocked on her door that day. I knew that in his midseventies he had single-handedly hauled a number of cedar logs down a mountain, cut and split them by hand, then built the nearly half-mile-long pasture fence I had just climbed over. And I knew that he had been one of nine young men from the state of Washington who shocked both the sports world and Adolf Hitler by winning a gold medal in rowing at the 1936 Olympics.

When Judy opened the door and ushered me into her cozy living room, Joe was stretched out in a recliner with his feet up, all six foot three of him. He had a thin white beard, and his eyes were puffy. An oxygen tank stood nearby. Rain flecked a window that looked out into the wet woods. A fire was popping and hissing in the woodstove. Jazz tunes from the 1930s and 1940s were playing quietly on the stereo.

Judy introduced me, and Joe offered me an extraordinarily long, thin hand. We talked for a while. Joe's voice was thin and reedy, not much more than a whisper. When the conversation began to turn to his own life, I leaned closer and took out my notepad. I was surprised at first, then astonished, at what this man had endured and overcome in his life. But it wasn't until he began to talk about his rowing career that he started, from time to time, to cry. He talked about learning the art of rowing, about the sleek and delicate wooden boats known as "shells," about tactics and techniques. He told stories about long, cold hours on the water under steel-gray skies, about smashing victories, and about marching under Adolf Hitler's eyes into the Olympic Stadium in Berlin. But it was when he tried to talk about "the boat" that the tears really welled up in his bright eyes.

At first I didn't know what he meant by "the boat." I thought he meant the *Husky Clipper*, the racing shell in which he had rowed his way to glory. Then I thought he meant his crewmates. Eventually I realized that "the boat" was something more than just the shell or its crew. To Joe, it was something bigger than that, something mysterious and almost beyond definition. It was a shared experience, a golden moment long ago, when he had been part of something much larger than himself. Joe was crying partly for the loss of that moment, but much more for the sheer beauty of it.

As I was preparing to leave that afternoon, Judy removed Joe's gold medal from the glass case against the wall and handed it to me. The medal had vanished once, years before. The family had searched high and low, then given it up for

A Washington crew working out, circa 1929.

lost before they finally found it, buried in some insulating material in the attic. A squirrel had apparently taken a liking to the glimmer of the gold and hidden the medal away in its nest. As Judy was telling me this, it occurred to me that Joe's story, like the medal, had been squirreled away out of sight for too long.

I shook Joe's hand and told him I would like to come back and talk to him some more. I said that I'd like to write a book about his rowing days. Joe grasped my hand again and said he'd like that, but then his voice broke once more. "But not just about me," he whispered. "It has to be about the boat."

The Washington shell house, 1930s.

# 1

## Only Nine Seats

On a sunny October afternoon in 1933, two young men, taller than most, hurried across the University of Washington's campus. The school was perched on a bluff overlooking the still waters of Seattle's Lake Washington. A gray, overcast morning had given way to a radiant day, and students were lounging on the grass in front of the massive new stone library, eating, chatting, and studying. But the two boys, both freshmen in their first weeks of college, did not stop. They were on a mission.

One of them, six-foot-three Roger Morris, had a loose, gangly build, dark hair, and heavy black eyebrows. The other, Joe Rantz, was a pencil tip shorter, but more solidly built, with broad shoulders, powerful legs, and a strong jaw. He wore his blond hair in a crew cut and watched the scene through gray eyes verging into blue.

The boys, who had recently met in engineering class, rounded the library

Seattle's Hooverville.

and descended a long grassy slope. They crossed Montlake Boulevard, dodging a steady stream of black automobiles. After a few more turns they followed a dirt road running through open woods and into a marshy area at the edge of Lake Washington. As they walked they began to overtake other boys headed in the same direction.

Finally they came to a point of land jutting out into the water. An odd-looking building stood there, an old airplane hangar covered with weather-beaten shingles and inset with enormous windows. The sides slanted up toward the roof. At the front, a wide wooden ramp stretched from enormous sliding doors to a long floating dock. Lake Washington spread out to the east. The canal known as the Cut stretched to the west, connecting to Portage Bay and the calm waters of Lake Union.

A crowd of young men, 175 in all, milled about nervously. They were mostly tall and lean, like Joe and Roger, though a dozen or so were noticeably short and slight. And they all shared the same goal. They wanted to make the University of Washington's freshman rowing team.

A handful of current team members, older boys wearing white jerseys emblazoned with large purple *W*s, stood with their arms crossed, eyeing the newcomers, sizing them up. Joe and Roger stepped inside the building. Along each wall of the cavernous room, the long, sleek racing shells were stacked four high on wooden racks. With their polished wooden hulls turned upward, they gleamed in white shafts of light that fell from the windows overhead. Faded but still colorful banners from rival colleges hung from the rafters. Dozens of spruce oars, each ten to twelve feet long and tipped with a white blade, stood on end in the corners of the room. The air was dry and still. It smelled sweetly of varnish and freshly sawn cedar. The sound of someone working with a wood rasp came from the back, up in a loft.

Joe and Roger signed in, then returned to the bright light outside and sat on a bench, waiting for instructions. Joe glanced at Roger, who seemed relaxed and confident.

"Aren't you nervous?" Joe whispered.

Roger glanced back at him. "I'm panicked. I just look like this to demoralize the competition." Joe smiled briefly, too close to panic himself to hold the smile long.

For Joe, more than anyone else there, something important hung in the balance that day, and it was more than a spot on the crew. He already felt as if he didn't fit in with most of the other students on campus. Most of the young men around him were city boys dressed neatly in freshly pressed woolen slacks and expensive cardigan sweaters. Their fathers were doctors and lawyers. They were mostly unbothered by the problems plaguing so much of the country that fall.

America was in the fourth year of the Great Depression. Ten million people had no job and no prospect of finding one. No one knew when the hard times might end. As many as two million people were homeless. In downtown Seattle that morning, hungry men stood in long lines waiting for soup kitchens to open. Others prepared to spend the day trying to sell apples and oranges for a few pennies apiece. Down by the waterfront, in crowded shantytowns, mothers huddled over campfires and children awoke in damp cardboard boxes that served as their beds.

Joe himself had been on his own for years, with no one at home to support him. Every day he wore the same old wrinkled hand-me-down sweater and the same dusty old shoes. He had worked for a year after high school to save up enough money to pay for his first year of college. Yet his savings were probably not going to last. If he ran out of money, there was a good chance he'd have to drop out of school, head back to his small, bleak hometown, and look forward to a life of odd jobs, foraging in the woods for food, and living alone in a cold, half-finished house. A spot on the freshman crew could prevent that. Each rower was guaranteed a part-time job on campus. That job might just bring in enough money to get Joe through four years of school. Then he could earn an engineering degree and find a good job. If all went well, he could marry his high school sweetheart, a bright, pretty girl named Joyce who stood by him no matter what.

But making the team was not going to be easy. Within a few short weeks, only a handful of the 174 boys gathered around him would still be contenders for seats in the first freshman boat. That was the one Joe felt he needed to be in to guarantee his place on the team. In the end, there were only nine seats in the boat.

Harry, Fred, Nellie, and Joe Rantz, circa 1917.

# 2

# A Dream Life Shattered

The path Joe followed down to the shell house that afternoon was only the last few hundred yards of a much longer, harder, and at times darker journey.

Joe was the second son of Harry Rantz and Nellie Maxwell. Harry was a big man, well over six feet tall, large in the hands and feet, heavy in the bones. He was a tinkerer and inventor, a dreamer of big dreams. In his spare time he loved to work with his hands and build contraptions of all kinds. He fiddled with machines, took apart mechanical devices in order to understand them. He even designed and built his own version of an automobile from scratch. Nellie Maxwell was a piano teacher and the daughter of a preacher. They had their first child, Fred, in 1899. Seven years later, looking for a place where Harry could make his mark on the world, they headed west from Pennsylvania, crossed the country, and settled down in Spokane, Washington.

The town was surrounded by ponderosa pine forest and open range country.

The summers were crackling hot, the air dry and perfumed with the vanilla scent of ponderosa bark. In the autumn towering dust storms would blow in from the wheat country to the west. The winters were bitter cold, the springs stingy and slow in coming. The Rantz family moved into a small frame house on the north side of the cold, clear Spokane River, and Joe was born there in March of 1914.

Harry set up an automobile shop. Each morning he rose at four thirty to go to work, and often he didn't return home until well after seven in the evening. It was hard work, but his business did well and he was able to buy his family nice things. Nellie taught piano to neighborhood children and doted on her sons, lavishing love on them and watching over them carefully.

On Sunday mornings the family attended church together, then spent the day relaxing. Sometimes they just walked into town to buy freshly made peach or strawberry ice cream. Sometimes they drove out to a nearby lake, where they could rent boats and explore the shoreline or spend a hot afternoon swimming or sitting on the grassy banks enjoying a picnic. But the best part for Joe was when they went to Natatorium Park in the cool shade of the cottonwood trees down by the river. Something interesting and fun was always going on there. They could watch a baseball game or listen to a John Philip Sousa band concert. What Joe particularly loved was when his parents would put him on the park's spectacular new carousel and he could ride, whirling around and around on the back of a carved tiger or elegant horse under the carousel's dazzling lights.

But when Joe was just about to turn four, this dream life shattered. His memories of what happened next were a kaleidoscope of broken images. He remembered his mother standing by his side in an overgrown field, coughing violently into a handkerchief, and the handkerchief turning bright red with blood.

Young Joe, age TK.

He remembered a doctor with a black leather bag. He remembered sitting on a hard church pew swinging his legs while his mother lay in a box at the front of the church and would not get up. He remembered lying on a bed with his big brother, Fred, perched on the edge. He remembered Fred talking softly about dying and about angels and about needing to go to college and about how Joe would have to go east to stay with relatives in Pennsylvania. He remembered sitting quietly alone on a train for long days and nights, with blue mountains and green muddy fields and rusty rail yards and dark cities full of smokestacks all flashing past the window by his seat. He remembered meeting a woman who said she was his aunt Alma and then, almost immediately, becoming terribly sick. He remembered lying for weeks in a bed in an unfamiliar attic room with the shades always pulled. No Ma, no Pa, no Fred. Only the lonely sound of a train now and then, and a strange room spinning around him. Plus the beginnings of a new heaviness, a feeling of doubt and fear pressing down on his small shoulders and congested chest.

As he lay ill with scarlet fever in the attic of a woman he did not really know, the world he had known back in Spokane dissolved. His brother had gone off to finish college. His mother was dead of cancer. His father had fled to Canada, unable to cope with his wife's terrible death.

A little more than a year later, in the summer of 1919, his brother called for him, and five-year-old Joe rode the train back across the country again all by himself. Although he was only twenty, Fred had married and found a good job, and he took care of his little brother for the next two years. By that point, their father,

Joe's mother, Nellie.

Joe with Harry, Thula, Mike, and Harry Jr. at the Gold and Ruby mine.

Harry, had returned from Canada, married a young woman named Thula La-Follette, and built a new house in Spokane.

For Joe, that meant still more change. Soon he was moving to another new home, living with a father he hardly remembered and a stepmother he did not know at all. But at least it was a real home, and in time this new life began to feel normal. The house was spacious and well lit. Out back there was a swing with a wide seat big enough for him and his father and Thula to ride three at a time on warm summer nights. He could walk to school, cutting through a field where he would sometimes snatch a sweet ripe melon for an after-school snack. He dug long, elaborate underground tunnels in the vacant lots nearby, and spent long cool afternoons in them escaping Spokane's searing dry summer heat. And the new house was always filled with music. Harry had kept Nellie's most precious possession, her piano, and he delighted in sitting at the keys with Joe. Harry pounded out popular tunes as his son, perched on the bench next to him, gleefully sang along. Although she was an accomplished violinist, Thula did not join in. She didn't like the often corny music Harry and Joe chose, and she was not particularly happy to have Nellie's piano in her house.

In January 1922, Harry and Thula had a boy named Harry Junior, and the following year they had another son, Mike. With his family growing and more mouths to feed, Harry had to take a job at a gold mine in Idaho some 140 miles away. He'd work there during the week, then make the long drive home on the weekends.

During one of these weekend visits, in the middle of a dark, moonless night, nine-year-old Joe suddenly awoke to the smell of smoke. He heard flames crackling somewhere in the house. He snatched up baby Mike, grabbed Harry Junior, and stumbled out of the house with his little half brothers. His father and Thula burst out of the house in singed nightclothes a few moments later. Once he saw that his boys were safe, Harry dashed back into the smoke and flames. Several minutes passed before he reappeared. With the fire raging behind him, he was pushing Nellie's piano inch by inch out through a garage door. He had risked his life to save the last thing he had left from his first marriage. Now, as Joe stood and watched their home burn to the ground, he had that same feeling he'd experienced in his aunt's dark attic years before. The same coldness, fear, and insecurity. Home, it was beginning to seem to him, was something you couldn't necessarily count on.

George Pocock, Rusty Callow (Washington coach before Ulbrickson), Ky Ebright, and Al Ulbrickson.

# 3

# A Thousand and One Small Things

The Washington shell house would eventually become a kind of home to Joe Rantz, but on the first day of practice he and the other freshmen did not even row. The afternoon was largely consumed by the collection of facts and figures. Joe and Roger and all the other hopefuls were told to step onto scales, to stand next to measuring sticks, to fill out forms detailing their medical backgrounds. Assistant coaches and older students carrying clipboards stood by, eyeing them and recording the information.

Few of the young men assembled outside the shell house that afternoon had ever rowed a stroke in their lives. Most of the freshmen were city boys, but a few, like Joe, were farm boys or lumberjacks or fishermen. They came from foggy coastal villages, damp dairy farms, and smoky lumber towns all over Washington state. Growing up, they had wielded axes and fishing gaffs and pitchforks, building up powerful arms and broad shoulders. They were strong, and the

Tom Bolles

Al Ulbrickson

coaches knew their strength would help those boys, but they also knew rowing was at least as much art as brawn. There were a thousand and one small things that had to be learned and performed in precisely the right way to propel one of those narrow shells through the water with speed and grace. Over the next few months, the few boys who made the team would need to master every last one of those thousand and one small things. And in those few months some essential questions would be answered. Would the farm boys be able to keep up with the intellectual side of the sport? Would the city boys have the toughness to survive?

The freshman coach, Tom Bolles, was in charge that day. He would be the one to decide which nine boys would make the first freshman boat. But another man stood quietly in the broad doorway of the shell house. He was tall, with cold slate-gray eyes, and he was dressed impeccably in a dark three-piece business suit, a crisp white shirt, a tie, and a fedora hat. His name was Al Ulbrickson, and he was the head coach of the rowing program. Ulbrickson was known as the least talkative man on campus. Some of the local sports reporters called him the "Man with the Stone Face." He did not like to show his emotions, but he knew the sport of rowing well. He had been the lead rower, or stroke oar, of a Washington crew that had won national championships in 1924 and 1926. The college had quickly hired him as a coach after graduation. Now rowing was the center of his life and almost a religion to him.

The new boys sauntered along the dock, getting a feel for the long, yellow-spruce oars. Many of the freshmen, Ulbrickson noted, looked fit. As a group, they were tall and moved gracefully. Ulbrickson was pleased by what he saw. When Bolles and his assistant coaches released the boys for the day, Joe Rantz and all the rest straggled up the hill toward the campus. They moved in small groups, shaking their heads, talking softly among themselves about their chances of making the team. Ulbrickson stood on the floating dock, listening to the lake water lap at the shore, watching the boys leave.

He was studying them closely because he was thinking well beyond the upcoming season. The previous year had been a strong one for the Washington team. They defeated their archrivals from the University of California, then beat out the best crews the East had to offer, including Yale, Cornell, and Harvard. But Ulbrickson was not satisfied. In 1932, a crew from California had won Olympic gold. No Washington coach had ever even come close to taking a team to the Olympics. The next Games were set to take place in Berlin, Germany, in 1936, and Al Ulbrickson didn't just want to get a crew there. He wanted to bring gold home to Seattle.

To pull it off, the coach knew, he was going to have to clear a series of imposing hurdles. He'd have to outsmart Cal coach Ky Ebright, who was widely regarded as the intellectual master of the sport. Ebright had an uncanny knack for winning the big races, the ones that really counted. Ulbrickson needed to find a crew that could beat Ebright's best when it mattered most. Then that crew would have to outrace the top boats from the East at the Olympic trials. Finally, if they did earn the right to represent the United States, they'd face the best oarsmen in the world. They would have to beat the British, who had practically invented the sport. The Italians, who had nearly won in 1932. And the Germans, who, under the new Nazi system, were said to be building extraordinarily powerful and disciplined crews.

Before he could get to Germany, though, Ulbrickson had to find the nine young men who would make up his crew. He wondered if any of those green and untested boys he had just watched on the dock might meet his strict qualifications. They'd need raw power, superhuman stamina, and solid intelligence to master the details of rowing technique. But they would need something else as well. Something even more important. To be part of that kind of crew—a gold medal crew—each young man would also have to be able to put aside his own personal ambitions. He'd have to throw his ego over the side of the boat, to leave it swirling in the wake of his shell. He'd need to pull, not just for himself, not just for glory, but for the other boys in the boat.

# 4

# Life in Exile

Joe Rantz was no stranger to pulling for himself. He'd been forced to do so at an early age. After the fire burned down their home, nine-year-old Joe and his family moved to the camp near the Idaho mine—the Gold and Ruby— where Joe's father worked. Harry Rantz no longer had to make the long drive back and forth, but their new home was a stark change from Spokane. The Boulder City camp consisted of thirty-five small cabins and a few other ramshackle buildings clinging to the side of a mountain. Wooden sidewalks stretched from one building to the next. A one-room schoolhouse stood on a flat spot among the pines, but there were few children, and the attendance was low. A rutted dirt wagon road plunged from the schoolhouse down the mountainside, cutting back and forth to the base before spilling onto a bridge across the Kootenai River. To Thula, it was a dismal place, but to young Joe, Boulder City was a wonderland.

When his father operated the mine's huge steam shovel, Joe could perch

The Gold and Ruby mine cabins.

happily on the rear end of the machine and ride it as it swung around in circles, almost like the carousel back in Spokane. His father built him a go-cart, and Joe dragged it up the steep roads to the top of the mountain. He pointed the cart downhill, climbed in, and released the brake. He raced down the road at breakneck speed, careening around the hairpin turns, whooping at the top of his lungs all the way to the river and across the bridge. Then he climbed out and began the long trek back to the top of the mountain and did it again and again. He didn't stop until it was too dark to see the road. When he was in motion, outdoors, the wind in his face brushed away all the anxiety that had been eating at him since his mother's death. He felt alive.

When winter closed in and the mountainside was deep in powdery snow, his father got out the welding equipment and built Joe a sled. With it he could rocket down the wagon road at even more terrifying speeds. Sometimes, when the adults weren't watching, he'd take Harry Junior up the mountain. Joe would find one of the railroad carts used to carry ore down the mountain, give it a shove, and then jump in with his little brother. The two boys would rattle down the tracks at terrifying speeds with Harry Junior in front, shrieking in delight.

When he wasn't hurtling down the mountain, Joe helped out at the mill, attended the one-room school above the camp, explored the woods, and climbed among the 6,400-foot-tall mountains in the national park nearby. He swam in the river and hunted for deer antlers and other treasures in the woods. At home, on a small plot of ground inside the picket fence surrounding his family's cabin, he tended his very own vegetable garden. But that little garden didn't produce nearly enough to satisfy Joe's hunger. He was growing fast, and he inhaled food as quickly as his stepmother made it. Thula worried constantly that her own boys, Harry Junior and Mike, wouldn't get enough to eat. And the household wasn't getting any smaller.

Thula was pregnant again, with her third child, and she was miserable living in that tiny cabin on the mountainside. She was beautiful, educated, and artistic. When she was young, growing up on a farm, she had been determined to seek a finer life when she left home. Now she was stuck in Boulder City. It was unbearably hot and dusty in the summer, wet and muddy in the spring and fall. Winter brought the worst of it. Come December bitterly cold air from Canada made its way through every crack and crevice in the walls of her flimsy cabin. It sliced through whatever layers of clothing she put on. She had hoped to become a concert violinist, but her beloved violin mostly sat on a shelf these days. Her hands were so cracked and sore from the cold, dry Idaho air that she could hardly hold the bow. She was still saddled with a screaming infant, a bored and complaining toddler, and a stepson who seemed to think of nothing but eating. It did not help that to pass the time Joe sat in the cabin and plucked incessantly at a ukulele, singing and whistling the corny songs that he and his father seemed to enjoy.

One warm summer afternoon, her tension and frustration finally boiled over. She was in the kitchen, shoving pans around the stovetop angrily while Joe was outside, down on his hands and knees, working in his vegetable garden. That little garden plot was a sanctuary for him. He was in charge of it, not Thula, and it was a source of enormous pride. When he could bring a fresh basket of tomatoes or an armful of sweet corn into the cabin, and then see them on the dinner table that night, he felt that he was contributing. He felt he was helping Thula, maybe making up for whatever he might have done lately to annoy her. That afternoon, as Joe was working his way down row after row, pulling weeds, he turned around to find his eighteen-month-old brother following him. Mike was imitating Joe, only he wasn't pulling weeds. He was plucking half-grown carrots out of the ground.

Joe turned and bellowed at him in rage.

Mike unleashed a long, wailing scream.

A moment later, Thula ran down the steps, red faced and seething. She snatched Mike up from the ground, whisked him into the cabin, and slammed the door behind her.

When Joe's father came home from work later that evening, Thula was waiting for him in the doorway. She demanded that he take Joe out back and whip him with a belt, but Harry merely took him upstairs and gave him a good talking-to instead. Thula exploded. She declared that she would not live under the same roof as Joe, that Harry must choose between him and her. She said Joe would have to move out if she were to stay in such a godforsaken place. Joe was only ten years old.

Early the next morning, Joe's father led him up the wagon road to the school-house at the top of the hill. He left Joe sitting outside on the steps and went in to talk to the male schoolteacher. Joe sat and waited in the morning sunlight. He drew circles in the dust with a stick and stared sadly at a Steller's jay. The bird had perched on a nearby branch and begun screeching at him. It seemed to Joe that even the bird was scolding him.

After a long while, his father and the teacher emerged from the schoolhouse and shook hands. They had struck a deal. Joe was to chop enough kindling and split enough wood to keep the school's huge stone fireplace stoked day and night. In return, he would have a place to stay. From now on, he was going to sleep at the school.

So began Joe's life in exile. His stepmother would no longer feed him, so every day he trudged down the wagon road to the miner's cookhouse for breakfast and dinner. The meals weren't free. Joe worked for the company cook, Mother Cleve-land. He carried heavy trays of steaming food from the cookhouse to the dining hall next door, where workers in dirty coveralls sat at long tables covered with white butcher paper. The plates were heaped high with hotcakes and bacon in the morning and with slabs of meat and potatoes in the evenings. The men talk-ed loudly and ate ravenously. As they finished their meals, Joe hauled their dirty dishes back to the cookhouse. In exchange for his efforts, Joe could eat all the bacon and hotcakes and meat and potatoes he wanted. In the evenings, after din-ner, he trudged back up the mountain to the schoolhouse to chop more wood, do his homework, and sleep.

caption TK.

The work and the food proved good for Joe in one way. He continued to grow rapidly in size and strength. The long treks up and down the mountain built up his legs. Swinging the ax at the schoolhouse sculpted his arms and shoulders. He ate all he could at the cookhouse, yet he still always seemed to be hungry for more. Food was never far from his thoughts. When the schoolteacher taught him how to find edible mushrooms out in the woods, Joe was thrilled at the notion that he could find food that others might walk by without even noticing.

Still, his world had again grown dark, narrow, and lonely. There were no boys his age in the camp. His best friends had been his father and Harry Junior. Now, living alone, he pined for the times when the three of them sneaked out behind the cabin to toss a ball around among the pine trees or to roughhouse in the dust. He missed how they used to pound out their favorite songs on the piano when his stepmother wasn't around. He missed the times he'd spent alone with his father, playing cards or tinkering with their big Franklin touring car. Most of all he missed the times he and his father would sit out at night on the cabin's porch and stare up into the astonishing swirls of stars shimmering in the black Idaho sky. They'd sit there, together, saying little, mostly just being together, breathing in the cold air, waiting for a falling star to wish upon. Sometimes his father would whisper, "Keep your eyes peeled. The only time you can't see one is when you stop watching." Sitting on the schoolhouse steps alone at night and watching the sky just didn't seem the same.

Freshmen on Old Nero.

# 5

# Making the Climb

After the first meeting at the Washington shell house, the real practices began. Every day, after classes, Joe made the long trek down to the lake. He donned his jersey and shorts. He weighed in, like all the boys, so the coaches could make sure they weren't gaining too many extra pounds or training so hard that they lost too much weight. Each shell held eight rowers, along with a coxswain (pronounced *kok-son*), a smaller boy who'd direct their pace and steer the boat. At every practice, the boys were split into training crews, so Joe checked a chalkboard to see which group he was assigned to for the day. Then he joined the others on the wooden ramp in front of the shell house, to hear what Freshman Coach Bolles had to say.

Tom Bolles was slim and young, with a bland, pleasant face. He was a former rower himself, and thanks to his habit of wearing wire-rimmed glasses, some sportswriters had nicknamed him "the professor." The name was appropriate, since he had to do as much teaching as coaching with these newcomers. In those first few weeks, Bolles began each session with a talk. He changed his topic each day, but Joe had begun to notice two common themes. First, the boys heard time and again that rowing was difficult almost beyond imagining. In the months ahead, Bolles said, their bodies and moral characters would be tested. Only those who possessed near superhuman physical endurance and mental toughness would prove good enough to wear a *W* on their chests. By Christmas break most of them would have given up, Bolles said, perhaps for something less demanding, like football.

But it would not be all pain and difficulty. Bolles also spoke of life-transforming experiences. He said the boys had a chance to become part of something larger than themselves. The best of them would tap into a strength and power they did not yet know they possessed. They'd grow from boys to men. At times Bolles dropped his voice a bit and talked of near mystical moments on the water—moments they would remember, cherish, and recount to their grandchildren when they were old men. Moments, even, that would bring them nearer to God.

To achieve that level of brilliance, however, they would first have to train their bodies and minds to endure brutal punishment. The major muscles in their arms, legs, and back had to be strong enough to propel the boat forward through the water, against the wind. At the same time, the smaller muscles in their necks, hands, wrists, and even feet would have to fine-tune their movements, adjusting their balance, controlling the oar, and ensuring that each motion was in tune with the seven other rowers in the boat. They'd risk injuries to their shoulders, knees, back, and more. Their palms would blister and bleed from pulling those long oars until their hands developed tough callouses.

And all that was merely what they could expect in practice. The competitive races would be the most brutal of all. There were no chances to cool off or drink water during a crew race. There were no time-outs. Their bodies would burn energy at a furious rate, a rate unlike that in almost any other sport. A single two-thousand-meter race was just as exhausting as playing two basketball games back-to-back. Yet all that effort would be packed into only six minutes. There was no question of whether they would hurt, or how much, Bolles said. The question was what they would do, and how well they would do it, when that pain struck.

During those first days, as the boys listened to Coach Bolles, they occasionally noticed a figure standing in the background. He was tall, in his early forties, and he wore horn-rimmed glasses. He spoke with a crisp British accent and his hair was dark and wavy, long on top, but cropped high around the sides and back, so that he seemed to be wearing a bowl atop his head. Many of the boys knew that he built racing shells in the loft upstairs, for Washington and also for rowing teams across the country. Typically he wore a carpenter's apron covered with red sawdust and curls of wood shavings. In time, they would find out that he was far more than a builder of boats. In fact, the heart and soul of much of what Coach Bolles was saying, the talk of those mystical moments on the water, had come from that mysterious figure in a carpenter's apron.

But the boys didn't have much time to wonder about the man. Once Coach Bolles finished talking each day, they wrestled the long, white-bladed oars from their racks, carried them down to the water, and prepared to row. They were not remotely ready to step into a delicate, sixty-two-foot-long racing shell. They would have capsized it and ended up in the lake. Instead they waited turns to board the school's training barge, *Old Nero*. The vessel was wide and flat-bottomed, with a long walkway running down the middle and eight seats for novice oarsmen on either side. All the rowers faced the back of the boat and sat on small seats that slid back and forth along greased runners. Since 1907, hundreds of hopeful freshman at the University of Washington had learned the basics of rowing in that old barge. Now it was Joe's turn.

As Joe and the boys flailed at their oars, Bolles and Ulbrickson strode up and down the walkway in their gray flannel suits and fedora hats. For now, Ulbrickson, the head of the rowing program, was just there to watch and look for potential talent for his Olympic dreams. He hardly said a word, but Coach Bolles barked at them continuously. He corrected how they gripped the oars. He urged them to straighten their backs, to bend their knees, to straighten their legs. One moment he'd tell them to pull harder, the next he'd order them to ease up. It was bewildering and backbreaking.

Training in *Old Nero* was not meant to be fun. The coaches used the heavy barge partly as a way to drive out the boys who lacked the toughness for crew. The boys strained and heaved and gasped for breath, but for all their efforts, *Old Nero* hardly moved through the ruffled waters of the lake.. As they tried to absorb the lessons, they lived in constant fear of making any of the many mistakes Coach Bolles kept pointing out to them. One was particularly frightening. If the blades of their oars entered the water too deeply, at the wrong angle, or out of time with the others in their crew, or if they remained in the water too long, the oar would suddenly become stuck. This was known as "catching a crab." When it happened, it felt as if some gargantuan crustacean had reached up from the depths and seized the blade. The boat kept moving, but the oar didn't. The boy who "caught the crab" might be smacked hard in the chest with the handle and knocked out of his seat. Or if he held on to the oar too long, he might be catapulted into the water. Every stroke he took offered each boy the possibility of a wet, cold, and spectacularly public form of humiliation.

Out of all the freshmen, the only one who'd ever rowed before was Joe's friend Roger Morris. As a boy he'd spent his summers rowing a small boat in Manzanita Bay, a lovely blue cove in western Washington. When he was twelve years old, he once rowed fifteen miles from his family's cabin outside Seattle to their house in the city, all because he had a terrible toothache and wanted to get home and see his mother. But aboard *Old Nero*, Roger Morris discovered that his experience was no help. His freewheeling style of rowing was nothing like the precise racing stroke that Coach Bolles was trying to teach.

None of the freshmen found the technique easy to master. The days grew shorter, the October nights colder, and still the workouts went on for three hours every afternoon. By the time the boys came in off the water, their hands were blistered and bleeding. Their arms and legs throbbed. Their backs ached and they were soaked with a mixture of sweat and lake water. They racked their oars, hung their rowing clothes up to dry, dressed, and began the long walk up the hill to campus.

Each evening, Joe noticed that fewer boys were making that climb. And he noted something else. The first boys to drop out were the ones with the fancy clothes and polished shoes. As Joe made his way to the shell house every afternoon, he saw more and more of those same boys lounging on the grass in front of the library. The hurting was taking its toll, and that was just fine with Joe. Hurting was nothing new to him.

Portrait of young Joyce.

# 6

# Another Chance at a Home

Joe's schoolhouse exile ended in November of 1924. When Thula gave birth to her first daughter, Rose, she demanded that the family leave Boulder City for good. So they picked up Joe at the schoolhouse, drove to Seattle, and moved into the basement of Thula's parents' home. With another infant to tend to, Thula was no happier in their cramped quarters here, though. Once again Joe always seemed to be in her way. So when Harry got a new job with a logging company a half-day's journey west of Seattle, Thula said Joe had to leave too. Harry took his son, still ten, to live with a family near the camp.

By 1925 Harry had saved enough money to buy an auto repair and tire shop in Sequim (pronounced *skwim*), a small town northwest of Seattle. Sequim sat on a wide expanse of prairie between the snowcapped Olympic Mountains and the broad, blue waters of the Strait of Juan de Fuca. The weather was dry compared to rain-drenched Seattle, so dry that early settlers had found cacti growing

Downtown Sequim

on the open prairies. Harry's shop was right downtown, and the whole family moved into a small apartment above it.

Joe enrolled in the Sequim school and spent his weekends tinkering with the cars in his dad's garage. When the mayor of Sequim accidentally smashed up Harry's car one day, he replaced it with a newer model, and Harry gave Joe his old Franklin so he could learn by repairing it. Another little girl arrived—Joe's half-sister Polly—and Harry bought some farmland outside town and began building a new house by hand.

The farmland was rough and raw, covered by hundreds of stumps from the forest that had recently been logged off. Joe and his dad began to dig up the stumps. They dug a ditch to divert water from the nearby Dungeness River to a waterwheel that Harry built. The waterwheel powered a sawmill that Harry also built. Then he felled some of the few trees still standing on the property and used the lumber to frame a two-story house. He and Joe collected smooth river rocks from the Dungeness and erected an enormous stone fireplace. The house was still only half completed when Harry sold the shop and moved everyone out to the farm. Over the next two years, the work continued. Joe and his dad built a wide front porch, a woodshed, and a ramshackle henhouse that soon became home to more than four hundred chickens. They constructed a rickety milking barn for half a dozen dairy cows. Joe's dad even figured out a way to use the waterwheel in the sawmill to generate electricity for lights in the house. On dark winter nights the lights flickered on and off depending on how much water was flowing through the waterwheel.

They never quite finished the house, but that made little difference to Joe. Once again he felt like he had a home. And he had a new world to explore. The meadow behind the house was covered with sweet wild strawberries in summer. The water flowing from the waterwheel formed a deep, wide pond, which became home to salmon and steelhead and trout that swam down the ditch from the Dungeness. Whenever Joe wanted fish for dinner, he simply took out a net, picked one out, and hauled it in. At night, as he lay in bed, he could hear bears splashing in the pond for fresh salmon and trout of their own. Sometimes he could hear cougars shrieking out in the dark woods.

At school, Joe became a popular and successful student. He was a particular favorite of Miss Flatebo, the music teacher. As the years passed, he acquired a collection of old, used stringed instruments, including a mandolin, several guitars, a ukulele, and two banjos. He'd play on the front porch after school, patiently mastering each instrument one by one. Soon he took to carrying one of the guitars onto the school bus. He'd sit in the back and play and sing as the other kids gathered around. There was one student in particular, a pretty girl named Joyce Simdars, who seemed to enjoy the music more than the rest. She had blonde curls, a button nose, and a fetching smile.

Joyce was a bright, intellectually curious girl brought up in a severely strict household. Her father was cold and distant, more likely to cuddle the family dog than one of his own children. He believed that hard work meant more than anything, and that no amount of it was too much. Yet it was her mother's unusual religious views that had the most powerful effect on Joyce. Her mother believed that there was only a "good Joyce." To her mother, the Joyce who misbehaved on occasion was actually an impostor. So, when Joyce did something wrong, she ceased to exist for her mother. This "bad Joyce" was made to sit on a chair in a corner and then was ignored completely until, mysteriously, the "good Joyce" finally reappeared. Confused, young Joyce would sit there in the corner, sobbing and checking on herself over and over again, thinking, "But I'm still here. I'm still here."

When Joyce first laid eyes on Joe Rantz, strumming his guitar in the back of the school bus, singing some funny old song and flashing his big white toothy grin, she was drawn to him immediately. And the first time Joe glanced up the school bus aisle and noticed this pretty girl coming toward him, his heart lit up. Soon she was sitting by his side every day, singing along with him in perfect harmony.

Joyce Simdars at sixteen.

Before long, though, life in the Rantz family began to sour once more. One winter morning Thula accidentally tripped and dropped an iron skillet full of hot bacon grease, potatoes, and onions. Harry Junior was lying on the floor and the skillet landed square on his chest. He and Thula screamed simultaneously. He ran out the door, and threw himself in a snowbank, but the damage was done. His chest was hideously burned and blistered. Confined to bed, he soon came down with pneumonia, and by the time he was well he had missed a year of school.

In the fall of 1929, Joyce Simdar's family home burned to the ground, while the family was away. Joyce was sent off to live for a time with family in Montana. The loss was a great one for Joe. All at once his morning bus ride to school was not what it had been. But much worse trouble lay ahead. A month after Joyce left, disaster struck Wall Street, the financial capital of the business world. The stock market crashed, triggering the Great Depression. Companies were destroyed across the country. Businesses and family farms collapsed. In Sequim alone, dozens of families simply walked away from their homes and farms, many leaving their dogs behind to fend for themselves. Just a week after the stock market crash, packs of these dogs began appearing daily on the Rantz family farm, chasing the cows, nipping at their legs. Soon the cows were too tired to give milk. Two weeks later, minks stole into the henhouse and slaughtered dozens of chickens, leaving their bloody corpses piled up in the corners. Joe's family had survived mostly by selling milk and eggs. Now they had little of either.

Then one rainy afternoon in November, the school bus dropped off Joe just as darkness was enveloping the house. Walking up the driveway, stepping over potholes full of rainwater, Joe noticed his father's car, its engine running. Something was tied to the roof, with a tarp over it. The younger kids were sitting in the backseat, among suitcases, and peering at him through steamy windows. Thula was sitting in the front seat, staring straight ahead. Joe's dad stood on the porch, watching him approach. Joe mounted the porch steps. His father's face was drawn and white.

"What's up, Pop? Where are we going?" Joe murmured.

Harry looked down at the boards planking the porch, then raised his eyes and gazed off into the dark, wet woods, looking over Joe's shoulder.

"We can't make it here, Joe. There's nothing else for it. Thula won't stay, at any rate. She's insisting."

"Where are we going to go?"

Harry turned to meet Joe's eyes.

"I'm not sure. Seattle for now, then California maybe. But, Son, the thing is, Thula wants you to stay here. I would stay with you, but I can't. The little kids are going to need a father more than you are. You're pretty much all grown up now anyway."

Joe froze. His gray-blue eyes locked onto his father's face, suddenly blank and expressionless, like stone. Stunned, trying to take in what he had just heard, unable to speak, Joe reached out a hand and laid it on the rough-hewn cedar railing, steadying himself. Rainwater dripping from the roof splattered in the mud below. Joe's stomach lurched. Finally he sputtered, "But can't I just come along?"

"No. That won't work. Look, Son, if there's one thing I've figured out about life, it's that if you want to be happy, you have to learn how to be happy on your own."

With that, Harry strode back to the car, climbed in, closed the door, and started down the driveway. In the backseat, Mike and Harry Junior peered through the oval rearview window. Joe could see Harry Junior mouthing words, "But what about Joe? What about Joe?" Joe watched the red taillights fade and disappear into a dark shroud of rain. He was fifteen years old, and he was on his own.

Joe with his banjo

# 7

# A Rare and Sacred Thing

As the first weeks of crew season wore on and the boys continued to toil aboard *Old Nero*, the weather turned raw and cold. Rain pelted their bare heads and shoulders. Their oars slapped against the wind-tossed waves, spraying icy water back into their faces, stinging their eyes. Their hands grew so numb that they could never be sure they had a proper hold on their oars. They could not feel their ears or noses. The cold lake beneath them seemed to suck warmth and energy out of them. Their aching muscles cramped up the moment they stopped moving. And the colder the weather got, the more boys gave up on crew. Even with most of the rich kids gone, Joe still stuck out among the survivors. He showed up every day in the same rumpled sweater, and almost every day the boys continued to make fun of it. He began going to practice early to change into his rowing clothes before the others arrived.

Joe and Roger slowly became friends. Most days Joe sat with him in the cafeteria. Occasionally they talked about their engineering classes. As often as not, though, they ate in silence. Roger didn't always say much, but there was a strand of affection and respect between them that Joe didn't feel with most of the boys in the shell house. It didn't really require a lot of talking.

For Joe and Roger, practice was only one part of a long, hard day. Roger walked two and a half miles to school each day from his parents' house, then slogged home again after classes and practice to help with family chores. On weekends, he played saxophone in a band at night for extra money. During the day he worked for his family's moving business, hoisting heavy sofas and beds and pianos in and out of homes all over town. This was often sad work, as he moved families out of houses they'd worked a lifetime to acquire and lost because of the Depression. Too often men stood hollow eyed and women wept in doorways as Roger loaded the last of their possessions onto a truck. But with businesses failing all over the country, and so many fathers and sons left without jobs, Roger was thankful his family had work at all.

After engineering classes each day, Joe hurried to crew practice, then on to his job in the student athletic store. He worked there until midnight, then trudged through the rain and the dark to the YMCA. In exchange for working as a janitor there, he was given a tiny, dark room in the basement. The room was part of what had been a coal bin, and it was just big enough for a desk and a bed. For Joe, the room represented little more than a place to do his homework and stretch out his aching frame for a few hours before heading off to classes again in the morning. It was not anything one could call a home.

By the end of October the original mass of hopeful rowers had been whittled down to eighty boys competing for a seat in the first two freshman boats. There would be a third boat and a fourth boat too, but the young men knew that practically nobody sitting in them would have a shot at making the top team—the varsity—the following year. On October 30 Coach Bolles decided it was time to move the best of them out of *Old Nero* and into shell barges. Both Joe Rantz and Roger Morris were picked to move up. Joe was bursting with pride the first time he sat down in one of the new boats.

The shell barges were easy to capsize and difficult to maneuver. Joe and Roger would have to learn an entirely new set of skills simply to remain upright. But these boats still weren't the sleek, narrow racing shells they'd row if they made the final team. Those boats happened to be some of the finest, fastest, most beautiful shells in the world, and they were built by hand right there in the Washington shell house. The man who shaped them, George Yeoman Pocock, was the same mysterious figure who'd been watching the boys so closely since their first meeting. And the reason he'd been studying them was that he knew as much about the fine art of rowing as he did about the art of building shells.

Pocock was all but born with an oar in his hands. Raised in England, within sight of some of the finest rowing water in the world, he was descended from a long line of boatbuilders. His father crafted shells for Eton College, just across the Thames River from Windsor Castle. Gentlemen's sons had been rowing competitively at Eton since the 1790s. At the age of fifteen, George began working alongside his father, laboring with hand tools to maintain and add to Eton's fleet. But he didn't just build boats; he also learned to row them, and to row them very well. At Eton, the coaches taught the boys to use long strokes, but George came to prefer the quick, powerful rowing style of the men who worked carrying passengers and freight on the Thames River. He adapted their style, inventing a more efficient stroke. Soon George and his brother, Dick, were outracing the aristocratic Eton boys, then giving informal rowing lessons to them after their classes.

When George was seventeen, his father entered him in a professional race and told him he could build his own boat for the contest from scrap lumber. He gave his son some advice that George never forgot: "No one will ask you *how long* it took to build; they will only ask *who* built it." So George took his time, carefully and meticulously handcrafting a single shell from Norwegian pine and mahogany. He won the race, defeating a field of fifty-eight oarsmen, and bringing home a large cash prize.

Late in 1910, his father lost his job at Eton. It was a crushing blow. The two brothers did not want to be a burden to their father, so they boarded a boat to Canada, where they heard it was possible to make a good living working in the woods. They traveled west to Vancouver and toiled at a series of dangerous jobs, one of which cost George two of his fingers. In 1912, the Vancouver Rowing Club heard of their reputation in England and paid them to build two single sculls, or boats for individual oarsmen. The brothers set up shop in an old, derelict shed floating out in the harbor. There, fifty yards offshore, they finally resumed what would be their life's work.

The shop was not ideal. Daylight showed through the roof. Rain shuddered through wide gaps between the wallboards. To bathe, every morning they dove out the window of their unheated bedroom and into the cold salt water of the harbor. At low tide the water receded and the shed sat on a mud bank. When the tide surged back in, the structure would remain stuck to the mud and gradually fill with water. Finally the mud would loosen its grip and the shop would burst back to the surface, water rushing out the doors at each end. Even in these conditions, the brothers built beautiful boats, and word of their craftsmanship soon spread in Canada and America.

One blustery gray day, George looked out the window of the floating workshop and saw a gangly and awkward man with a shock of reddish but graying hair flying in the wind. He was flailing his oars, not making progress in any direction. He looked, George thought, "like a bewildered crab." Dick thought he must be drunk. Eventually the brothers snagged the man's boat and dragged it alongside the workshop. When they helped him aboard, he grinned, stuck out a large hand, and boomed out, "My name is Hiram Conibear. I am the rowing coach at the University of Washington."

Conibear had become Washington's coach because nobody else was available to take the job, not because he knew the first thing about rowing. But he'd heard about the brothers, and he wanted a few of their long, sleek, elegant shells for the team, so he had made the journey to Vancouver. Soon the Pocock brothers moved down to Seattle and set up a new workshop at the University of Washington. George began to watch the Washington oarsmen on the water and quickly spotted problems in their technique. At first he held his peace. But when Conibear began to ask the Pococks for their opinion about his boys' rowing, George gradually spoke up. He began to teach the coach the more efficient style he'd developed in England, and the changes soon resulted in Washington's first significant victories. Before long, the other schools were taking note of the style, trying to figure out how something so different could be so successful.

Conibear died just a few years later, in 1917, when he climbed too far out on a limb while reaching for a plum in a tree in his backyard, and plunged headfirst to the ground. By then, however, Washington had become a serious contender in the college rowing world, and the coaches that followed Conibear came to rely on George for more than his boats. His brother, Dick, moved east to build shells for Yale, but George remained at Washington. Over the years, he watched many powerful and proud boys try to master the sport. As he studied and worked with them and counseled them, he learned much about the hearts and souls of young men. He learned to see hope where a boy thought there was no hope. He saw the power of trust, the strength of the affection that sometimes grew between a pair of young men. Or among a boatload of them striving honestly to do their best. And he came to understand how those almost mystical bonds of trust might lift a crew to another place, where nine boys somehow became one thing. A thing that was so in tune with the water and the earth and the sky above that, as they rowed, effort was replaced by ecstasy. It was a rare thing, a sacred thing. And George Yeoman Pocock, the man who'd been watching Joe and the other hopeful freshmen, knew more about it than anyone.

# 8

## Going It Alone

Rain was still pounding the roof of the half-finished house in Sequim when fifteen-year-old Joe woke up alone the morning after his family left him. A wind had come up during the night, and it moaned in the tops of the fir trees behind the house. Joe lay in bed for a long time, listening, remembering the days he spent lying in bed in his aunt's attic in Pennsylvania listening to the moaning of trains in the distance. The same fear and loneliness he felt then was weighing on him again, pressing down on his chest. He did not want to get up, did not really care if he ever got up.

Finally, though, he crawled out of bed, made a fire in the woodstove, put water on to boil, fried some bacon, and made some coffee. Very slowly, as he ate the bacon and the coffee cleared his mind, the spinning in his head began to lessen. He found himself creeping up on a new realization. It surprised him, but he opened his eyes and seized it, took it in, understood it all at once. He was sick and tired of finding himself scared and hurt and abandoned and endlessly asking himself why. Whatever else came his way, he wasn't going to let anything like this happen again. From now on, he would make his own way. He would find his own route to happiness, as his father had said. He'd prove to his father and to himself that he could do it. He wasn't going to be a hermit and live completely alone. Friends, he knew, could help him push away the loneliness. But he would never again let himself depend on them, nor on his family, nor on anyone. He would survive, and he would do it on his own.

He made some oatmeal and sat back down to think some more. His father had always taught him that there was a solution to every problem. But he had always said the sometimes the solution wasn't where people would ordinarily expect it to be. You might have to look in unexpected places and think in new and creative ways. He could survive on his own, he figured, if he just kept his eyes open for opportunities.

Over the next few weeks and months, Joe began to fend entirely for himself. He drove iron stakes into the ground to defend the chicken coop against future mink attacks and treasured the few eggs he gathered every morning. He foraged in the dripping woods for mushrooms, gathered the last of the autumn's black-berries, netted the last of the fish from the pond. He picked watercress for salads. Watercress and berries would only go so far, though. He knew he was going to need some money in his pocket. So he drove downtown in the old Franklin car his father had left behind, parked, and sat on the hood playing his banjo in the rain, hoping for spare change. In 1929, though, there was no such thing as spare change. Jobs and money were hard to find in towns like Sequim. People held on to every penny they had. His only audience consisted of a few stray dogs who sat on their haunches watching him idly and scratching their fleas. The only human who paid him any attention was a bearded character everyone called the Mad Russian, a man who had been wandering Sequim's streets barefoot and muttering to himself for as long as anyone could remember.

Joe dug deeper into his imagination for another way to earn money. Months before, he and his friend Harry Secor had discovered a spot on the Dungeness River where huge Chinook salmon lay in a deep, green, swirling pool. Some were as much as four feet long. Joe found a gaff hook in the barn, hid it in his pocket, and ventured up to the spot one misty Saturday morning with Harry. They worked their way through a tangle of cottonwood trees lining the Dungeness, dodging the game warden who patrolled the river. The boys cut a stout pole from a tree branch, lashed the gaff hook to it, and then stealthily approached the swift, cold river. If they were caught, there would be big trouble. The rules of fishing were strict. You were only allowed to catch the salmon with a proper hook and a line. The pole and hook the boys had devised was illegal, but Joe was desperate.

He took off his shoes, rolled up his pants, and waded quietly into the shallows upstream from the pool. When Joe was in position, Harry started throwing large river rocks into the pool and beating the surface with a stick. In a panic, the fish dashed upstream toward Joe. As they flashed by, Joe aimed the gaff at one of the largest of them, thrust the pole into the water, and deftly snagged the fish under the gills. Then he stumbled out of the water and dragged the thrashing salmon up onto the gravel bank.

Joe feasted on salmon that night, alone in the house. Then he set about turning the snagging of salmon into a business. Each Saturday afternoon he hiked the three miles into town with one or more of the enormous salmon slung over his shoulder, their tails dragging in the dust behind him. He sold the fish for cash or traded them for butter or meat or gas for his car.

Later that winter Joe discovered another way of making some cash. And again it wasn't exactly legal. Under the Prohibition laws, selling alcoholic drinks was illegal in 1929, but men called "bootleggers" made a living by sneaking liquor into the country and selling it to their customers. Joe discovered that a bootlegger named Byron Nobel was making the rounds in Sequim every Friday night, quietly leaving bottles behind particular fence posts. Joe learned to follow Nobel's big black car around town on dark, frosty nights, and swipe the bottles before the Nobel's customers could get to them. In their place Joe left bottles of dandelion wine he and Harry Secor brewed up in Joe's barn. Then Joe quietly sold the liquor to his own list of satisfied customers.

When he wasn't catching salmon or stealing booze, Joe threw himself into any kind of legitimate work he could find. He dug tunnels under tree stumps in his neighbors' pastures and pried them out of the earth with long iron bars or packed dynamite under them and blew them sky-high. He stooped and scraped with a shovel, digging irrigation ditches by hand. With a long-handled, doubled-edged ax, he split fence rails from massive cedar logs. He dug wells and built barns, crawling around in the rafters pounding nails. He lugged 120-bound cans of milk and sweet cream around dairy farms.

As summer came on, he labored under pale blue skies in the dry fields, cutting hay, forking it into wagons, and hoisting it by the ton into the lofts of his neighbors' barns. Later, he found work helping his older neighbor, a logger named Charlie McDonald. Together, Joe and Charlie worked a seven-foot two-man saw back and forth across the trunks of immense cottonwood trees. Sometimes it took an hour or more for them to fell a single tree. Then they lopped off all the branches with axes and pried the bark from the logs with long iron bars. Finally they harnessed them to Charlie's draft horses so they could be dragged out of the woods and sent to a pulp mill. Later, Joe found a more enjoyable way to make a few dollars when he and two of his school friends formed a band. With Joe on the banjo, they played during intermissions at the movie theater and at dances in nearby towns. They seldom made much money, but their performances got them into the theaters and dance halls for free.

Often now he would take his dinner with the McDonald family, which was better than eating in solitude, sitting at one end of the large table where his family used to gather for boisterous dinners. But at the end of the day, he was always alone, back in the big, empty, half-finished house. Sometimes he plinked at the keys of his mother's old piano and floated simple melodies through the dark, empty spaces of the house as the lights powered by the water wheel flickered on and off. Other times he sat on the front steps and played his banjo and sang quietly to himself late into the night.

There was one bright spot in Joe's lonely life. Joyce Simdars had returned from Montana. Joe often invited her to the Chicken Coop, Sequim's most popular dance hall, but she was rarely allowed to go, and only when her mother could accompany her. In many ways, Joyce's heavily supervised life could not have been more different from Joe's completely independent one. While her father worked outside tirelessly, her mother assigned her endless chores inside. She was always washing dishes, scrubbing floors, and wiping windows, even though she detested

Joe and Joyce at the beach

housework. She would much rather be outside, working in the vegetable garden or tending to the animals with her father. She liked how farmwork often involved solving practical problems or making something new. She loved to take things apart and see how they worked. That appealed to her intellectual curiosity. She was already a great student, interested in everything from photography to Latin to logic.

Although she understood that Joe's life had been hard and lonely, to Joyce, he seemed the very embodiment of freedom. She saw in him a window to a wider, sunnier world. He made his own rules, played his silly songs, and wandered in the woods at will, finding food or things he could use. But best of all, he seemed to care for her just as she was—to Joe there was no "good Joyce" or "bad Joyce." Just "Joyce," and that was enough. Many girls, she knew, would turn away from a boy as poor as Joe. But not her. She decided that someday she would make up for the way the world had so far treated Joe Rantz.

In the summer of 1931, Joe received a letter from his older brother, Fred, now a chemistry teacher at Roosevelt High School in Seattle. Fred wanted Joe to come live with him and his family and complete his senior year of high school at Roosevelt. If he did well at Roosevelt, Fred said, Joe just might be able to get into the University of Washington. Joe was wary. After nearly two years of struggle, he was finally beginning to get his feet under himself, to make it on his own. He did not want to leave Joyce either. But the prospect of studying at a great high school, and possibly moving on to the university, was just too exciting to pass up. He boarded up the farmhouse, promised Joyce he'd be back at the end of the school year, and moved in with Fred.

For the first time in as long as he could remember, he found himself with three square meals a day and little to do except attend school and explore his interests. He excelled in the classroom and quickly worked his way onto the dean's honor roll. He sang and performed in plays and made music. He signed up for the men's gymnastics team and proved to be a standout on the rings, the high bars, and the parallel bars.

One spring day in 1932, as he was practicing on the high bar in the gym he noticed a tall man in a dark gray suit and a fedora standing in the doorway and watching him intently. The man disappeared, but a few minutes later Fred walked into the gym and called Joe over to the door.

"A fellow just came into my classroom and asked who you were," Fred said. "Said he was from the university. He gave me this. Said you should look him up when you get to the U. That he might be able to use a fellow like you."

Fred handed Joe a card, and Joe glanced down at it:


ALVIN M. ULBRICKSON

HEAD COACH, CREW

UNIVERSITY OF WASHINGTON ATHLETIC DEPARTMENT


Joe pondered the card for a moment, then walked to his locker and put it in his wallet. It couldn't hurt to give it a try. Rowing couldn't be any harder than cutting cottonwoods.

# 9
## Part of a Single Thing

After graduating with honors from Roosevelt High School, Joe returned to Sequim as he'd promised Joyce. He planned to work for a year to scrape together enough money for a year's rent and books and tuition. First he got a job with the Civilian Conservation Corps, laying asphalt for the new Olympic Highway at fifty cents an hour. The money was decent, but the work was brutal. For eight hours a day, working under a hot summer sun, he shoveled steaming asphalt out of trucks and raked it out flat in advance of the steamrollers. On weekends he dug irrigation ditches and cut hay for local farmers. That winter he went back to cutting down cottonwoods with Charlie McDonald. All of the work was hard, but there was a saving grace. Joyce was in her last year of high school, and when she got off the bus each day, she would rush through the woods. Seventy years later, as an old woman, she would remember how when she hugged him he smelled of wet wood and the sweet wildness of the outdoors.

One radiant day in late April, he led her through a cottonwood grove to a small meadow on the bank of the Dungeness. Joe loved to find four-leaf clovers for Joyce. She was mystified at how easily he found them, but he always told her that it wasn't a matter of luck at all. The trick was simply keeping your eyes open. "The only time you don't find a four-leaf clover," he liked to say, "is when you stop looking for one." When he told her to sit and wait for a moment, she figured he was looking for one of those tokens of his affection. After a short while, shorter than usual, Joe returned.

"Found one," he said, beaming.

He held out a closed fist, and she reached out to receive the clover. But as he slowly unfolded his hand, she saw that it held not a clover but a golden ring with a small but perfect diamond sparkling in the rare spring sunshine.

After she graduated, Joyce moved to Seattle to be near Joe and attend the university herself. She had no intention of living a life like her mother's, where endless housework limited the horizons of her worldview. She wanted to live a life of the mind, and the university was her ticket to that life. Like Joe, she needed to work to stay in school, and despite her bright mind the only job available to her was the one she detested most: housework. After two weeks of unsuccessful interviews, she knocked on the door of a gaunt-looking elderly gentleman, a prominent local judge. There was a long, awkward silence as he stared at her after she'd stated her case. Finally he croaked, "Come back in the morning, and we'll see if you fit in the last maid's uniform."

The uniform fit, and with that Joyce had landed a job and a place to live. Now, on weekend evenings, when they both could get some time off, she and

Joe and Joyce in Seattle.

Joe could board a streetcar and go downtown to catch a movie. They danced at Club Victor on Friday nights, then attended college dances in the school's gymnasium on Saturday nights. Joe longed to bring Joyce to the swank, fancy places downtown that many of her friends frequented. Those more expensive spots had glittering chandeliers and pink walls painted with tropical scenes and polished dance floors capable of holding five thousand people at a time. You could dress up in fancy clothes and dance all night to popular bands' music at such places. It pained Joe that he couldn't afford that kind of date, but Joyce swore she didn't care. Sometimes for dates they just met at the student cafeteria, where they ate soda crackers and mixed ketchup with hot water and called it tomato soup.

On the afternoon of November 28, the last practice day of the fall term, the freshmen took one final, frigid workout. When the last boat had returned to the shell house, Coach Bolles told the boys to stick around. He said that it was time to announce who had made the first and second boats. Then he ducked into Al Ulbrickson's office.

The boys glanced at one another. Through the steamy windowpanes of the glassed-in office they could see the two coaches hunched over a desk in their flannel suits, studying a piece of paper. Now that the rainy season had begun, the shell house reeked sourly of sweat and damp socks and mildew. The wind shook the massive sliding door. As the two coaches lingered, the normally talkative boys turned uncomfortably silent. The only sound was a soft tapping. Up in the loft at the back of the room, Pocock was nailing together the frame for a new shell. Roger Morris drifted over and stood quietly next to Joe, toweling his hair dry.

Finally Coach Bolles emerged from the office and climbed up onto a bench, clutching the piece of paper. The boys shuffled into a semicircle around him.

He began by saying that this selection was not final. All of them could continue to compete for the seats he was about to announce. Nobody should get all swell headed just because he heard his name called out now. Nobody should think he was a sure thing. There wasn't any such animal. Then he began to read off the names on the list. He moved first through the assignments for the second boat.

When Coach Bolles finished, Joe glanced at Roger. His friend was staring morosely down at the floor. Neither of them had been called. Then Coach Bolles began calling out the first-boat assignments: "Bow seat, Roger Morris. Number two seat, Shorty Hunt. Number three seat, Joe Rantz." As Bolles continued, Joe clenched his fist at his side and gave it a subtle little pump. Next to him, Roger began to exhale softly.

As the rest of the boys headed for the showers, those selected for the first boat took a shell barge off its rack, hoisted it over their heads, and marched it down to the darkening lake for a celebratory row. A light but cutting wind ruffled the water. As the sun set, they began to row westward, seeking the calmer waters of Lake Union.

The temperature had fallen into the upper thirties, and it felt even colder on the water. Joe hardly noticed. As the boat slipped onto the surface of Lake Union, the noise of city traffic fell away, and he entered into a world completely silent except for the rhythmic barking of the coxswain, calling out their pace from the stern. Joe's seat slid methodically and silently back and forth on the greased runners beneath him. His arms and legs pulled and pushed smoothly, almost easily. When the white blade of his oar entered the black water, it did not splash. It just murmured.

At the north end of the lake, the coxswain called out, "Way... nuff!" The boys stopped rowing. The shell glided to a stop, the long oars trailing in the water alongside them. The boys sat without talking, breathing heavily, exhaling plumes of white breath in the darkness. Even now that they had stopped rowing, their breathing was synchronized, and for a brief, fragile moment it seemed to Joe as if all of them were part of a single thing, something alive with breath and spirit of its own. Joe gulped huge drafts of the frigid air and sat staring at the city lights in the distance—the amber lights of downtown, the ruby-red lights of radio towers, the green lights on docks along the shore. He watched the scene turn into a soft blur of colors as tears filled his eyes. For the first time since his family had left him, Joe began to cry.

He turned his face to the water, fiddling with his oarlock so the others would not see. He didn't know where the tears had come from, what they were all about. But something inside him had shifted, if only for a few moments.

The boys had caught their breaths, and they were talking softly, not joking for a change, not horsing around, just talking quietly. Then the coxswain called out, "Ready all!" Joe turned and faced the rear of the boat, slid his seat forward, sank the white blade of his oar into the oil-black water, tensed his muscles, and waited for the coxswain's next command, the one that would propel him forward into the darkness, and his future.

The coxswain called out again, "Row!"

# 10

# A Broken Machine

In January, after a trip back to Sequim for Christmas break, Joe and Joyce returned to Seattle. When crew practice started up on January 8, Joe and the seventeen other boys in the first and second freshman boats learned that they could now abandon the shell barges and step for the first time into proper racing shells, the sleek and lovely cedar craft built by George Pocock.

They also learned that what had seemed a brutal workout schedule in the fall was merely a whisper of what the coaches had in mind for them now. In the next few months, they were told, they would race mostly against one another and the upperclassmen on the team. Joe's spot was not guaranteed. Nobody's was. The boys would continue to fight for the top eight seats. In mid-April just one boatload of freshmen would face their primary rival, the University of California at Berkeley right here on Lake Washington. If they prevailed in that race—and only if they did so—they would likely earn a chance to compete against the elite eastern schools for the national freshman championship

George Pocock at work in his shop.

in June. The whole season would come down to just two major races.

In his six years as freshman coach, Tom Bolles had never coached a crew that had lost a race to California, or anyone else, on Lake Washington. Bolles didn't intend for this bunch to be the first. But they had some catching up to do. The boys at Cal had been rowing since late August, and racing against each other in real shells since late October, when Joe and the boys had only begun trying out the shell barges. From now until race day, Bolles told his boys, they would row six days a week.

It was a cold, wet winter in Seattle. Day after day it rained, but day after day they rowed anyway. They rowed through cutting wind, bitter sleet, and occasional snow, well into the dark of night. They rowed with cold rainwater running down their backs, pooling in the bottom of the boat, and sloshing back and forth under their sliding seats. It was nearly as wet above the surface of the lake as below. Through it all, Bolles followed them back and forth across Lake Washington, riding through the slop and chop in the open cockpit of his brass-trimmed, mahogany-planked motorboat, the *Alumnus*. Wearing a bright yellow rain slicker, he bellowed commands at them through his megaphone until his voice grew hoarse and his throat sore.

Once again, boys began to give up, climbing wearily back up the hill after practice and refusing to come back for more. While all the boys in Joe's boat stuck it out, the easy camaraderie they felt the first time they went out together in November quickly evaporated. Anxiety, self-doubt, and bickering replaced that first night's good feelings. Bolles scrutinized them, trying to figure out who to keep in the first boat and who to demote. By mid-spring he found himself struggling daily with the freshmen. "They seem to be getting slower every day," he complained.

One of the fundamental challenges in rowing is that when any one member of a crew goes into a slump, the entire crew goes with him. Each of the rowers has a slightly different role, depending on his position in the boat, and each of these roles is critical. The oarsman sitting in the first seat, nearest the bow, has to be strong, but more than anything he has to be technically sound. One wrong move and he can disrupt the course, speed, and stability of the boat. The same is true to a lesser extent of the rowers in the two and three seats. The four, five, and six seats, often called "the engine room" of the crew, have to be the biggest and strongest rowers. The rower in the seventh seat has to be nearly as strong as those in the engine room but also alert, constantly aware of and in tune with what is happening in the rest of the boat. The "stroke oar," who sits in the eighth seat, faces the coxswain. Theoretically, the stroke rows at the rate and with the degree of power called for by the coxswain. He is supposed to do what he is told. But in the end it is the stroke who controls these things. Everyone else in the boat follows the stroke. When working well, the entire boat operates like a well-lubricated machine, with every rower serving as a vital link in a chain that powers it forward.

This machine can break down easily. A lack of concentration on one person's part can impact the performance of the whole boat. To keep themselves focused, the freshman crew in Joe's boat had come up with a mantra that their coxswain, George Morry, chanted as they rowed. Morry shouted, "M-I-B, M-I-B, M-I-B!" over and over to the rhythm of their stroke. The letters stood for "mind in boat." The chant was meant as a reminder that from the time an oarsman steps into a racing shell until the moment the boat crosses the finish line, he must keep his mind focused on what is happening inside the boat. His whole world must shrink down to that small space.

Unfortunately, no amount of chanting could break the freshmen's slump, so Bolles had to wonder if there were weak links in that chain. One potential weak link seemed to be Joe Rantz. Coach Bolles had tried moving Joe back and forth between the number three seat and number seven, but with no effect. The problem looked to be technical. From the beginning of tryouts, Bolles had not been able to get Joe to "square up" consistently. To square up, a rower has to rotate his oar so that the blade is perpendicular to the surface just before he inserts it into the water on the catch, the beginning of each stroke. If the angle is wrong, the rower cannot produce enough power, and the whole boat suffers a loss of speed. Squaring up requires strong wrists, and Joe just couldn't seem to get the hang of it. Beyond that, his stroke was generally eccentric. He rowed powerfully but decidedly in his own way, and his own way looked to be largely ineffective.

Bolles yanked Joe out of the first boat one afternoon, and the boat slowed down. Perplexed, he put Joe back in, and Joe and the crew beat the second boat by a decisive margin. Bolles was flummoxed. Maybe the problem wasn't in Rantz's wrist. Maybe it was in his head.

Bolles didn't know the answer, but for Joe, the brief incident was a sudden and cold reminder. He could easily lose his position on the crew. His place at the university was not secure either. Everything he had worked for could be over on any given afternoon.

Rowing into the Montlake Cut.

# 11

# The Makings of
# Something Exceptional

Joe continued to feel like everyone's poor cousin. He still had to wear his ragged sweater to practice almost every day, and the boys still teased him continuously for it. "Hobo Joe," they snickered. "You trying to catch moths with that thing?" One evening in the cafeteria, they found a new way to laugh at his expense. Joe had piled his plate high with meat loaf and potatoes and creamed corn. He attacked the food with his knife and fork, shoveling it into his mouth. The moment he had cleared his plate he turned to the boy next to him, asked him for his leftover meat loaf, and devoured it just as rapidly.

Over the noise of the cafeteria, he didn't notice that someone had come up behind him. Nor did he hear the snickering. When he finally paused, he turned around to find half a dozen fellows from the shell house holding their dirty plates out to him, grins smeared across their faces. Joe paused, startled and humiliated, but then, with his ears growing red, he turned around, put his head down, and resumed eating. He was hungry nearly all the time, and he wasn't about to walk away from perfectly good food because of a bunch of jerks in jerseys. He'd dug too many ditches, cut down too many cottonwoods, foraged in the cold, wet woods for too many berries and mushrooms.

By the end of March, the freshman slump appeared to be over, and Joe had secured his spot in the number three seat. On April 6, after a windy week had kept the boys off the water, Coach Ulbrickson decided to hold a race between all his crews, including the varsity, junior varsity, and freshmen boats, out on Lake Washington. He gave the JV crew a head start of three boat lengths because they'd been rowing so poorly. He told the freshman crew to end its race at the two-mile mark, the standard distance for freshman races. The varsity and junior varsity were to continue racing to the three-mile mark.

Ulbrickson lined the boats up and barked, "Ready all . . . row!" through his megaphone. Harvey Love, the varsity coxswain, was talking and missed the signal. The freshmen immediately leapt out a half boat length ahead of the older boys. For a mile the boats held their stroke rates and positions. The junior varsity was three boat lengths out in front. The freshmen were in second. The bow of the varsity boat was locked in place alongside the freshman boat's number five seat. Then, slowly, the varsity's bow fell back to the six seat, the seven seat, the stroke seat, and finally the coxswain's seat. By the mile-and-a-half mark, the freshmen had opened a sliver of water between the rear of their boat and the varsity's bow.

Then they started to close on the junior varsity, despite their head start. Normally a crew would increase its pace to catch a boat in the lead, but so far the freshmen had not raised their stroke rate at all. A quarter mile remained in the race and coxswain George Morry knew his crew had plenty left in the tank.

Finally he told them to kick the stroke rate up a couple of notches. They surged past the junior varsity and into the overall lead. When they reached the two-mile mark, they were two full lengths ahead of both other boats. Morry shouted, "Way 'nuff," and the freshmen pulled up, let their oars ride the water, and coasted to a stop. As the other two boats finally passed them, the freshman boys pumped their fists in the air.

Bolles looked down at his stopwatch, saw the freshmen's two-mile time, and looked again. He had known they were getting sharp, but now he knew that he had the makings of something exceptional in his boat. What he didn't know was whether they were fast enough to beat California.

On the day of the Pacific Coast Regatta, Friday, April 13, the weather was near perfect. Joyce Simdars joined fourteen hundred other boisterous students dressed in purple and gold, the school's colors, as they boarded a ferry to watch the competition from the water. The university's marching band was already aboard. As the band played fight songs, the brass instruments blaring and the kettle drums rattling, Joyce settled on a bench on the foredeck, sipping coffee in the sun. She was looking forward to watching Joe. She had taken a rare afternoon off from her live-in job at the judge's house. She needed the break. She detested the job. She had always loathed housework, but now she had to wear a ridiculous uniform and creep around the house as quietly as a dormouse, lest she disturb the judge. Now, sitting on the ferry, she was nervous for Joe, since she knew how much staying on the crew meant to him, but she was happy to be out of the house, out in the fresh air and bright sunlight. The band changed over to jazz tunes and students began to dance out on the main deck.

As the time for the races grew near, people on private docks, backyard decks, and grassy slopes all along the lakeshore spread out blankets, pulled lunches out of picnic hampers, and tested out their binoculars, ready to watch. Hundreds of boats began to form a semicircle around the finish line. Two thousand more fans clambered aboard an observation train. The sides of the train cars were open, so as the train ran parallel to the racecourse, the riders could watch the races from beginning to end. All told, nearly eighty thousand people had come out to watch the races. The university's football stadium didn't even hold that many fans.

The Washington and California freshman crews would go first, for a distance of two miles. Out on the lake, Joe sat in the number three seat; Roger Morris sat in the number seven seat. Both were nervous, as were all the boys. They had plenty of reason to be anxious. Warm as it was onshore, a moderately stiff north breeze had sprung up out in midlake, and they would be rowing directly into it. That would slow their time and perhaps cramp their style. In the next few minutes each of them would need to take more than three hundred strokes. And if one of them missed just one of those strokes and caught just one crab, the race would effectively be over, their season in ruins. Joe surveyed the crowd assembled along the shoreline. He wondered whether Joyce was half as nervous as he was.

At 3:00 p.m., the Washington freshmen paddled their shell parallel to California's, did their best to settle their minds into the boat, and waited for the start signal. The bow of the boat drifted slightly to one side and George Morry, Washington's coxswain, raised his right arm to signal that his boat was not quite ready to row.

The boys straightened the bow. The band on the ferryboat stopped playing. The students stopped dancing and crowded near the rails. Thousands along the shoreline raised binoculars to their eyes. The starter called out, "Ready all!" The Washington boys slid their seats forward, sank their white blades into the water, hunched over their oars, and stared straight ahead. George Morry lowered his right arm. Grover Clark, the Cal coxswain, did the same. The starter barked, "Row!"

California exploded off the line, rowing furiously and surging a quarter length ahead of Washington's bow. Having seized the lead, Cal dropped its stroke rate. Washington was rowing even fewer strokes per minute, but held its position just behind Cal. All the boys had their minds fully in the boat now. Facing the stern, the only thing any of them could see was the heaving back of the oarsman in front of him.

As they passed the quarter-mile mark, the two boats slowly came even. Then Washington began to overtake California, methodically, seat by seat. The Washington boys were still rowing at a remarkably low rate, but by the one-mile mark, they had open water on Cal. Their confidence surged. The pain in their arms and legs did not much bother them. They felt almost invulnerable.

In the Cal boat, Grover Clark screamed out, "Gimme ten big ones!"—the standard call in rowing for ten mammoth strokes, as hard and powerful as each oarsman can muster. But Washington remained out in front by two boat lengths. At the mile-and-a-half mark, Clark called for another big ten, but by now Cal's boys had given everything they had to give. Washington's boys still had more. As they entered the last half mile, the headwind died down. Cheers began to rise from the semicircle of boats ahead, the beaches, and the train. The loudest of all rose from the ferryboat full of students. Ahead by four lengths, George Morry finally called for a higher stroke rate, and Washington sliced across the finish line four and a half lengths ahead of California, and almost twenty seconds ahead of the freshman course record.

Shrill horns and cheers resounded all along the shores of Lake Washington. The freshmen paddled over to the California boat. In a rowing race, the victorious crew traditionally had the right to collect the jerseys of their vanquished rivals. So Joe and the boys accepted the shirts off the Cal crew's backs, shook their hands, and paddled off, exultant. The real celebration began when the boys were dropped off at the student ferry. Beaming, Joe bounded up the steps, searching for Joyce. At five foot four, she was hard to find in the surging crowd. Joyce had seen him, though. She worked her way through until she finally emerged before Joe. He promptly leaned over, wrapped her in a sweaty hug, and lifted her off her feet.

When the band began to play dance tunes again, Joe, barefoot in his jersey and shorts, took Joyce and twirled her once under his long, outstretched arms. Then they danced, careening around the deck, swinging, smiling, and laughing, giddy under a blue Seattle sky.

# 12

## Almost Without Pain

Seven weeks later, on the evening of June 1, 1934, the University of Washington's marching band and more than a thousand fans crammed into the ornate marble lobby of the King Street railroad station in Seattle. They cheered and sang fight songs as the freshman and varsity crews boarded a Great Northern train, the *Empire Builder*, on their way to the national championships in Poughkeepsie, New York.

Joe and the freshman boys were in particularly high spirits. Few of them had ever been outside of Washington; most had never been on a train. For the most part, they'd been brought up milking cows and swinging axes and stacking lumber. They knew the first names of half the people in the towns they came from. Yet here they were, about to cross the entire continent.

As he sat in his plush seat, looking out through the green-tinted train window, Joe could not quite believe the celebration spilling from the lobby out onto the platform. He'd never been celebrated for anything, and yet here he was, a part of something that people didn't just admire but adored. It filled him with pride but also with a strained unease. It brought up the kinds of things he tried not to think about these days.

That evening, as the *Empire Builder* climbed over the Cascade Mountains and set out across the arid wheat country of eastern Washington, the boys played cards, told jokes, and raced up and down the aisles of the train, tossing a football. The next day, they filled balloons with water, positioned themselves on the clattering platforms between coaches, and hurled them at any available target—cows grazing in fields, dusty cars waiting at clanging railroad crossings, sleeping dogs sprawled on platforms in small-town stations. Each time they hit a target they sang the fight song "Bow Down to Washington" as they rumbled past their astonished victims.

Later Joe pulled out his guitar and tuned it. He'd been nervous about bringing it along, but the mood was right, and he felt close to his teammates now. He began to strum chords and sing, launching into the camp tunes and cowboy songs he'd played in high school.

At first the boys just stared at him. Then they began to glance at one another, then to snicker, and finally to hoot and holler. "Lookee there at Cowboy Joe!" one shouted. Another called down the aisle, "Hey, boys, come and hear Rantz, the rowing troubadour!" Joe looked up, startled, and stopped playing. Red faced but with his jaw set and his eyes stone cold, he quickly fumbled the guitar back into its case and walked to a different part of the train.

Few things could have been more hurtful for Joe. His music had brightened the bleakest days of his boyhood. It had drawn people to him in high school, made him friends, and even helped him earn a few dollars in Sequim. Thanks to music, he'd gotten to know Joyce. Music was his special talent, a particular point of pride. Now, suddenly and unexpectedly, it had turned on him. Just when he was beginning to feel part of something larger than himself, he felt cast out again.

The first athletic competition of any kind between two American colleges was a rowing race pitting Harvard against Yale in 1852. As the years passed, rowing became more popular, and other eastern colleges launched crew programs. In 1895, the Intercollegiate Rowing Association held its first regatta at Poughkeepsie, on a straight four-mile stretch of the Hudson River. Soon, the regatta came to be seen as the most prestigious crew race in the country, the equivalent of a national championship, and it was immensely popular with fans. In 1929, as many as 125,000 people came out to watch it in person. Millions more listened to the radio coverage. The regatta rivaled the Kentucky Derby, the Rose Bowl, and the World Series as a major national sporting event.

For most of the first quarter of the century, the eastern colleges thoroughly dominated the races in Poughkeepsie. By the 1920s, the western crews from Washington and California had begun to claim occasional victories over powerhouses like Cornell and Syracuse. Still, for the thousands of wealthy easterners who sailed their yachts up the Hudson to watch the regatta each June, it remained a natural assumption that the East would once again resume its proper place atop the rowing world. Eastern fans were accustomed to seeing the sons of senators and governors and titans of industry sitting in racing shells—not farmers and fishermen and lumberjacks.

The economic hardships of the last few years had only sharpened the distinction between the eastern boys and Washington's freshman crew. The Great Depression had ruined the westerners' families and hometowns, but many of the eastern rowers were from another class, the wealthy and privileged few who went on living in luxury despite the rest of the country's troubles. So the 1934 regatta was not just another boat race. It was shaping up to be a clash of eastern privilege and prestige on the one hand and western sincerity and brawn on the other. In some ways, it was going to be a clash of rich and poor.

This was clear enough when the Washington crews moved into their temporary boathouse in New York, a dilapidated old shed on the Hudson. It was drafty, rickety, sitting on thin stilts over the river. The showers pumped foul-smelling cold water directly from the Hudson over the boys' heads. Their lodgings were not much better. In the attic of a nearby boarding house, they were crammed six to a room. They struggled to sleep on cots that seemed more like torture racks than beds.

As if that wasn't bad enough, they'd also been rowing terribly. After their victory over California, Joe and the freshman crew could not seem to maintain any sort of consistency. They rowed sloppily. On one occasion, before leaving for the regatta, they nearly collided with a tugboat. Coach Bolles threatened to replace some of them with substitutes, but then watched them turn in a stunning time on a windy, choppy day on the lake. His confidence was restored, but when they arrived in Poughkeepsie, and Bolles hurried them down to the Hudson to practice, they faltered again.

The weather was oppressively hot and sticky, unlike anything the boys had experienced back home. By the time they carried their shell, the *City of Seattle*, down to the water, they were already drenched in sweat. The boys rowed at a warm-up pace until Bolles lifted his megaphone and told them to take it up to a sprint. They leaned into their oars, but Bolles didn't even bother to look at his stopwatch. He could see at a glance that they were rowing well off their best pace. Worse, they looked ragged, clearly done in by the heat.

River rowing was new to them. They could handle almost any amount of wind and chop on Lake Washington, but the waves on the Hudson were different. These were long, low waves that hit the boat from the side. The effects of tide and the river's current baffled them. They weren't used to the water moving under their boat, pushing them places they did not intend to go, and they wandered from one side of the course to the other. Frustrated, Bolles shouted, "Way 'nuff!" through his megaphone and waved the boys back to the shell house.

Race day, Saturday, June 16, dawned clear and warm. Fans began to arrive by train and by automobile from all over the East. All afternoon trolleys rattled down the bluff on the steep Poughkeepsie side of the Hudson River, transporting fans to the waterside. A gray heat haze hung over the river. White electric ferries made their way back and forth, shuttling fans over to the west side, where an observation train awaited them. By 5:00 p.m., more than seventy-five thousand people lined both banks of the river, sitting on beaches, standing on docks, perched on roofs, bluffs, and walkways. Fans sipped lemonade and fanned themselves with copies of the program. The river was jammed with yachts at anchor, their teak decks crowded with race fans, many of them wearing crisp nautical whites and royal-blue caps with gold braid. Canoes and wooden motorboats darted in and out among the yachts. A gleaming white coast guard cutter and a gray Navy destroyer were anchored at the finish line. Only the seven racing lanes in the middle of the river remained clear and open water.

The freshman race was set to go off first, over a two-mile course. As the shells approached the starting line, the coaches' boats fell in behind their crews. Their engines sputtered and gurgled, white exhaust fumes burbling from the water behind them. The smell of diesel fuel hung faintly over the river. Washington was in lane three, right next to the Syracuse Orange in lane two. The Orange had won three of the last four freshman titles. They were the defending champions and clear favorites.

The heat had barely faded. A hint of a north wind lightly ruffled the water. The Washington boys backed their shell into position. Morry, the coxswain, lowered his hand to signal the starter that his boat was ready to row. Joe Rantz took a deep breath, settling his mind. Roger Morris adjusted his grip on his oar.

At the crack of the starting pistol, Syracuse immediately jumped in front, rowing at thirty-four strokes per minute, followed closely by Washington, rowing at thirty-one. Everyone else—Columbia, Rutgers, Pennsylvania, Cornell—began to fall behind. At a quarter of a mile down the river, it looked as if Syracuse would, as predicted, settle into the lead. But by the half-mile mark, the boys from Washington had crept up and nosed ahead without raising their stroke rate. They'd begun to get a feel for rowing in the current. They were too focused on their task to notice the heat. As the leaders swept under the railroad bridge at the halfway mark, officials on the bridge signaled that Washington was in the lead.

Slowly the bow of the Syracuse boat came into Joe's field of view, just beginning to fall away behind him. He ignored it, focused instead on the oar in his hands, pulling hard and pulling smoothly, rowing comfortably, almost without pain. At the mile-and-a-half mark, someone in the middle of the Syracuse boat caught a crab. The Orange faltered for a moment, then recovered their rhythm.

But it no longer mattered. Washington was two and a half lengths ahead. Cornell, in third, had all but disappeared, eight lengths farther back. George Morry whipped his head around, took a quick look, and was startled at the length of their lead. Nevertheless, as he had against California in April on Lake Washington, he called up the rate in the last few hundred feet, just for the show of it. The boys from Washington passed the finish line an astonishing five lengths ahead of Syracuse.

In Seattle and in Sequim, people who had been huddled around radios in their kitchens and parlors stood and cheered. Just like that, the farm boys and fishermen and shipyard workers from Washington State, boys who just nine months before had never rowed a lick, had whipped the best boats in the East and become national freshman champions.

And it wasn't just folks back home who stood up and paid attention to what had just happened. The win startled race fans across the country. It wasn't just the margin of victory or their time. It was how the boys had rowed the race. From the starting gun to the finish, they had rowed as if they could keep going at the same pace for another two miles or ten. At the finish, rather than slumping in their seats and gasping for breath, they had been sitting bolt upright, looking calmly around. They looked as if they were simply out for an afternoon paddle, wide-eyed western boys, wondering what all the fuss was about.

Ky Ebright

# 13

## Stay Out of Our Life

**The regatta did not end** as well as it started for Washington. After the freshman crew's stunning victory, Coach Ulbrickson's varsity lost to California. The Olympic Games were still two years away, but Ulbrickson was left staring at a cold, hard fact. His rival at Cal, Ky Ebright, just seemed to have an uncanny knack for winning the ones that mattered most. That very evening, the national newspapers began to carry stories saying that certainly the boys from Cal would be going to the Olympics in 1936.

Joe took a roundabout journey home from Poughkeepsie. He visited his aunt and uncle in Pennsylvania, then traveled down to New Orleans, marveling at the sight of the huge ships making their way up the Mississippi, eating huge platters full of cheap shrimp and crab, digging into steaming bowls of gumbo and jambalaya, soaking up the jazz and the blues. On his way home, he traveled across an America that had begun to dry up and blow away.

It was the beginning of what would come to be called the "Dust Bowl." Intense heat was scorching crops across the country. A colossal dust storm had swung out of eastern Montana, rolled east, dumped twelve million tons of dirt on Chicago, and then moved on to tower over Boston and New York. People in New York's Central Park stood and looked up in astonishment at a blackened sky. Somewhere in the neighborhood of 350 million tons of American topsoil had become airborne in that single storm. As Joe traveled north and west, staring out train windows, it seemed as if the whole country had withered and browned under the searing sun. Deep piles of powdery dust lay along fence lines. Windmills stood motionless. Gaunt cattle, their ribs protruding and their heads hanging low, stood listless at the bottoms of dried-up ponds. Under the fierce sun, people raised their hands to their brows and stared at Joe's train as it passed, giving it cold, hard looks, wishing they could get aboard and go somewhere else. Anywhere else.

That summer, Joe moved back to the half-finished house in Sequim, desperate to conjure up enough money to get through another school year. He cut more hay, dug more ditches, and spread more hot, black asphalt on the highway. He tried snagging salmon again too, but the game warden sneaked up on him from behind one day, slamming a piece of driftwood against the back of Joe's head and knocking him cold. He came to a few moments later, just in time to see his friend Harry Secor chasing the warden down the river with a pole. The boys got away, but they knew the warden would be back, so they never snagged a salmon again.

Mostly, Joe worked in the woods with Charlie McDonald. One afternoon Charlie took Joe upriver, hunting for cedar for a new roof on his farmhouse. The upper reaches of his property had been logged for the first time just a dozen years before. The loggers had taken only the prime middle section of each tree, leaving long sections from the tops, where the branches were, and the bottoms, where the trunks began to flare out and the grain of the wood no longer ran perfectly straight and true. Some of the cedars had been more than two thousand years old, and the stumps that remained were seven or eight feet in diameter and just as tall. They rose from the ground like ancient monuments.

Charlie led Joe among the stumps and downed trees, teaching him how to understand what lay beneath the bark of the fallen logs. Much of the wood could still be used, but only if one knew how to read the wood, to decipher its inner structure. Charlie rolled them over, felt for hidden knots and irregularities. He crouched down at the cut ends and peered at the annual growth rings. Joe was fascinated, intrigued by the idea that he could learn to see what others could not see in the wood. He was thrilled at the notion that something valuable could be found in what others had passed over and left behind.

Within a few days, Joe had mastered the tools used to cut and split the massive logs. A year of rowing had made his arms and shoulders strong, and he worked his way through the cedar like a machine. Proud of his new skill, he found that shaping cedar satisfied him down to his core and gave him peace. He liked the way that the splitting wood murmured to him before it parted, almost as if it was alive. As the wood opened up, it always perfumed the air, and the spicy-sweet aroma that rose from freshly split cedar was a familiar one from the shell house in Seattle.

A few years earlier, Pocock had made the revolutionary decision to begin crafting the skins of his rowing shells out of native Washington cedar. Pocock found the wood to be light, springy, and strong. He believed that his cedar shells had a kind of liveliness, a tendency to spring forward with each stroke in a way that no other design or material could duplicate. To Pocock, there was magic in cedar, an unseen force that imparted life to the shells he built.

Now, out in the woods, the scent of the freshly split logs brought Pocock to Joe's mind. Joe had been thinking a lot about Pocock lately. The man was mysterious, but it seemed to Joe that there was a connection between what the boatbuilder did in his shop and what he was trying to do himself, here among a pile of freshly split cedar, striving to master a skill, striving to become truly excellent at something difficult.

When Joe arrived back at at the shell house on October 5, 1934, it was another radiant afternoon, much like the day when he had first shown up as a freshman. But there was a different attitude among the bunch of boys Joe had rowed with last year. As they moved in and out of the shell house, in shorts and jerseys, helping Coach Bolles register the new freshmen, there was an unmistakable hint of swagger in their step. After all, they were the national freshman champions. Now, as sophomores, it was their turn to grin at the nervous freshmen climbing awkwardly aboard *Old Nero*.

There were other reasons to be confident. Over the summer, there had been suggestions that Ulbrickson should elevate them to varsity status immediately, even though juniors and seniors usually made up that first crew. It seemed profoundly unlikely, but the idea was out there, in public, and the sophomore boys already had begun to talk quietly about it among themselves. Ulbrickson had been thinking about it as well, but the last thing he needed was for a bunch of upstart sophomores to start thinking they were God's gift to rowing. They were good, but they were still green, not yet great. A *great* oarsman needed a rare balance of ego and humility. For now, what he saw strutting around the shell house and lounging in the doorway was plenty of ego and not much humility.

Coach Bolles had told Ulbrickson to look particularly hard at a couple of the boys. One was the baby of the boat, a seventeen-year-old boy in the number two seat, six-foot-three George "Shorty" Hunt. He was an ox for work and absolutely indispensable. But he was high-strung, nervous, someone you often had to treat with kid gloves to settle down, like a racehorse. The other was the blond kid with the crew cut in the number three seat, Joe Rantz. Ulbrickson remembered him as the boy he had spotted in the gym at Roosevelt High two years before. He was as poor as a church mouse. Anybody could tell that just by looking at him. When he wanted to, though, Bolles had reported, Joe Rantz would row longer and harder than any man in the boat. The problem was that he didn't always seem to want to. All last spring he had been on one day, off the next. He had learned to square up, but he marched to his own drummer. The others boys had taken to calling him "Mr. Individuality." He was physically tough, independent, confident, friendly, and yet at the same time strangely sensitive. He seemed to have tender spots that you had to watch out for if you wanted him to come through for you, though nobody, not even the other sophomores, could figure out quite what they were.

But Al Ulbrickson wasn't one to waste a lot of time trying to figure out a touchy kid's tender spots. He picked up the megaphone and barked at the sophomores to assemble down on the ramp. The boys shuffled toward the water. Ulbrickson stood higher on the ramp, so he'd be looking down at even the tallest boys. He gazed out at them for a moment, saying nothing. And then he began to tell them how it was going to be.

"You will eat no fried meats," he began abruptly. "You will eat no pastries, but you will eat plenty of vegetables. You will eat good, substantial, wholesome food—the kind of food your mother makes. You will go to bed at ten o'clock and arise punctually at seven o'clock. You will not smoke or drink. . . . And you will follow this regimen all year round, for as long as you row for me. . . . You will not use profane language in the shell house, nor anywhere within my hearing. You will keep at your studies and retain a high grade point average. You will not disappoint your parents, nor your crewmates. Now let's row."

Two weeks later, Ulbrickson listed the first tentative "boatings," or crew rosters, for the new year. There were five potential varsity boats in all. Most were made up of a mix of sophomores, juniors, and seniors. Only one boat from the previous season remained intact. Joe's boat, with Shorty Hunt at the two seat, and Roger Morris at seven. But lest anyone—and particularly the sophomores themselves—read too much into it, Ulbrickson put the boat far down the list. The sophomore boys were not in the first boat or the second. Ulbrickson placed them fifth.

As the fall training season got under way, the boys' swagger promptly disappeared from their steps. Ulbrickson was a harder man than Bolles, and this season would clearly be harder than the last. Joe in particular struggled to keep up his spirits. It wasn't just the status of his boat that worried him. It wasn't just the brutality of the long workouts or the days of rowing in the rain and bitter cold. Despite the long summer of work, Joe found himself even poorer than he had been the previous year. He could hardly afford to take Joyce out on dates of any kind now.

There were family matters eating at Joe as well. He had found out that Harry and Thula, and his half siblings, were living in Seattle. They had been there all along, in fact, since the night in 1929 when they had driven away and left Joe behind in Sequim. Over the years they had moved from home to home. First they lived in a dilapidated shed by the waterfront, with rats scurrying around the two rooms. Harry could not find work, and when they moved to a different house, it was hardly an improvement, as they could not even afford firewood to fuel the one stove that heated the house. Thula had to frequent local soup kitchens, looking for free food. Most of the meals she managed to put before her children consisted of thin stews made from parsnips, rutabagas, potatoes, and chipped beef.

When Harry finally landed a decent job as a mechanic, he moved the family to a small but respectable house, not far from where Joe rowed nearly every afternoon. That's where Joe found them in the fall of 1934. His brother Fred had given him the address, and Joe and Joyce drove over one afternoon. They parked, took deep breaths, and climbed a flight of concrete steps to the front porch, holding hands. They could hear someone playing violin inside. Joe knocked on a yellow Dutch door, and the violin fell silent. A shadow moved behind lace curtains on the upper half of the door. There was a moment's hesitation, and then Thula opened the door halfway.

She did not seem particularly surprised to see them. Joe had the sense that she'd been expecting this for a long time. She glanced at Joyce and nodded at her pleasantly enough, but she made no move to invite them in. There was a long moment of silence. Joe thought Thula looked careworn and exhausted, much older than her thirty-six years. Her face was pale and drawn, her eyes a bit sunken. Joe focused for a moment on her fingers and saw that they were red and chafed.

Finally Joe broke the silence. "Hello, Thula. We just came by to see how you are doing."

Thula peered at him silently for a moment, her expression veiled, then dropped her eyes as she began to speak.

"We're fine, Joe. We're doing fine now. How is school going?"

Joe said it was going well, that he was on the crew now.

Thula responded that she had heard that, and that his father was proud of him. She asked Joyce how her parents were doing, and expressed her regret when Joyce replied that her father was quite ill.

Thula continued to hold the door just half open, her body blocking the entrance. Even as she addressed them, Joe noticed, she continued to look down at the porch, as if studying something at her feet, trying to find the answer to something there.

Finally Joe asked if they could come in and say hello to his father and the kids. Thula said that Harry was at work and the kids were visiting friends.

Joe asked if he and Joyce could come back and visit them another time.

Thula seemed suddenly to find what she had been looking for. She raised her eyes abruptly and leveled them at Joe. "No," she said, her voice colder now. "Make your own life, Joe. Stay out of ours." And with that she closed the door gently and slid the deadbolt into position with a soft, metallic click.

As they drove away, Joyce fumed. Over the years she had been slowly learning more about Joe's life, about what had happened at the Gold and Ruby mine, and in Sequim. She could not understand how Thula had been so cold, how his father had been so weak, and why Joe himself seemed to show so little anger about it all. Finally, as Joe pulled over to the curb to drop her off at the judge's home, Joyce erupted. Why did he go on pretending they hadn't done him any harm? What kind of woman would leave a boy alone in the world? What kind of father would let her do that? She was nearly sobbing by the time she finished.

She glanced across the seat at Joe, and saw at once, through a blur of tears, that his eyes were full of hurt too. But his jaw was set, and he stared ahead over the steering wheel rather than turning to look at her.

"You don't understand," he murmured. "They didn't have any choice. There were just too many mouths to feed."

Joyce thought about that for a moment, then said, "I just don't understand why you don't get angry."

Joe continued to stare ahead through the windshield.

"It takes energy to get angry. It eats you up inside. I can't waste my energy like that and expect to get ahead. When they left, it took everything I had in me just to survive. Now I have to stay focused. I've just gotta take care of things myself."

George Pocock's shop

# 14

## Driven Nearly to Madness

The boys sat on hard benches, shivering in their mismatched shorts and cotton jerseys. The sun had already set, and the shell house was drafty and uncomfortable. Outside, it was a bitterly cold night. The panes of glass on the great sliding doors were frosted at the corners. It was the evening of January 14, 1935, the first crew turnout of the new year. Tensions in the shell house had run high during the fall season, as the continuing rumors that the sophomores might be pegged for the first varsity boat had everyone on edge. There was little of the usual banter and joshing. Icy stares began to replace good-natured grins. Now the boys were waiting for Al Ulbrickson to lay out his plan for the upcoming racing season. After a long, uncomfortable wait, Ulbrickson emerged from his office and began to talk. By the time he finished, nobody in the room was cold any longer.

He had started off simply, announcing a change of basic strategy. They were not going to take it slow for the first few weeks of winter quarter, as they general-ly did, working on details of form and technique while waiting for the weather to improve. Instead, they were going to row all out every day, right from the start. They were going to work themselves into top physical condition. And their races would be for the highest of stakes. This was not going to be an ordinary season. "At one time or another," he declared, "Washington crews have won the highest honors in America. They have not, however, participated in the Olympic Games. That's our objective." The push to go to Berlin in 1936, and to win gold there, was to begin that night.

Ulbrickson began to grow animated, almost emotional. There was more potential in this room, he said, than he had ever seen in a shell house in all his years of rowing and coaching, more than he ever expected to see again in his lifetime. Somewhere among them, he told the boys, was the greatest crew that Washington had ever seen. Maybe the best Washington would ever see. Nine of them, he ended up declaring, as if it were a certainty, were going to be stand-ing on the medal podium in Berlin in 1936. It was up to each of them whether they would be there or not. When he finished, the boys leapt to their feet and cheered.

The next morning the *Seattle Post-Intelligencer* exulted, "A New Era in Washington Rowing. Possible Entry in the Olympic Games in Berlin!"

All-out war promptly broke out in the shell house. The rivalries that had aris-en during the fall season now turned into outright battles. Accidental bumping of shoulders turned into open pushing matches. Locker doors were slammed.

Curses were exchanged. Grudges were nursed. Two brothers in different boats now barely greeted each other with grunts each afternoon.

The weather stalled Ulbrickson's plans to have the boys row themselves into shape. A series of brutal winter storms roared in from the Gulf of Alaska. Bitter winds ripped the surface of Lake Washington into a furious tumble of white-capped waves. The temperatures dropped into the teens, snow flurries turned into light snowstorms, which in turn became full-scale blizzards. When the boys did hit the water for quick sprints, they'd row in the snow until their hands grew so numb they could no longer hold the oars.

In February, the boats begin to compete head-to-head to see which crew would be the first varsity squad. Joe remained in the all-sophomore boat. Another member of his crew, Bob Green, had begun to annoy some of the boys in the other boats. Green had the habit of getting excited and bellowing encouragement to his crewmates during races. Normally, only the coxswain shouts commands, and this breach of an unstated rowing rule irritated the older boys, particularly Bobby Moch, the savvy little coxswain of the best JV boat.

Moch learned to turn Green's loudness to his advantage. Whenever his boat came up alongside Joe and the sophomores, Moch quietly leaned toward his stroke oar and told him to pick up the pace. Green meanwhile would be hooting and hollering at his own crew, urging them on. Moch would direct his megaphone over to the sophomore boat and say, "Well, Green just opened his big mouth again. Let's pass them!" By the time he said this, his own boat would already be starting to surge, since he'd secretly given the order to increase the pace. To the sophomore boat, though, it seemed like magic. The change appeared to be instant, as if Moch's crew could just blow past them anytime they wanted. Green would start yelling even more loudly, "More, more!" "Give me ten big ones!" But Moch's boat would already be accelerating away.

Each time Moch tried the trick, the sophomores lost their cool. They flailed at their oars, angry and desperate to catch up. Time after time, they got, as Moch called it, "all bloody nosed." And none more so than Joe. The whole thing seemed like another joke at his expense, designed to show him up. But it always worked.

Ulbrickson was starting to have some serious doubts about the sophomores. He had expected that by now they would emerge decisively as the new varsity lineup. But as he watched them struggle against the JV boys, they just didn't look like the crew that had won with such astonishing ease at Poughkeepsie. He studied them for a few days, trying to figure it out, looking for individual faults. Then he called Roger Morris, Shorty Hunt, Joe Rantz, and two other boys into his office for a talk. He told them flat out that they were all in danger of falling out of contention for the first varsity boat if they didn't shape up. Among other things, they were letting their emotions climb into the boat with them. They were losing their cool over little things, and that had to stop. He reminded them that there were only eight seats for rowers in the first varsity boat and that four or five boys were vying for each one. Then he stopped talking and simply pointed at the door.

Joe, Roger, and Shorty came out of the shell house shaken, trying to ignore a cluster of seniors and juniors smirking at them from the doorway. They started up the hill in the rain. Talking over what had just happened, they were beginning to get agitated.

Shorty Hunt had grown up in a small town. His family life had been stable, and as a result he'd grown up confident and highly accomplished. In high school he starred in three sports and excelled in the classroom, graduating two years early. He was talkative and good-looking, with wavy dark hair, and although he stood six foot three, his fellow students dubbed him "Shorty." He liked to dress well and was forever drawing admiring glances from the young women around him. He and Roger had been buddies from day one, and Joe was grateful that the two of them had never given him a hard time about his music or his clothes. In fact, more and more Joe could count on Shorty and Roger to come to his side when the older boys teased him or when Ulbrickson singled him out for criticism. Shorty rowed in the number two seat, right behind Joe, and he'd taken lately to looping an arm over Joe's shoulder whenever he seemed down and saying, "Don't worry, Joe. I've got your back."

As they walked up the hill from the shell house that night, the three boys complained about Ulbrickson. They were angry he'd chewed them out. Shorty, in particular, was agitated. Ulbrickson was unfair, he complained. He was a cold taskmaster, too hard on them, too blind to see how hard they were working. He'd do better to give a fellow an occasional pat on the back than to always find fault. Roger moped along, looking even more morose than usual. They all knew Ulbrickson wasn't likely to change. They agreed that from now on, they'd all better be watching one another's backs. That night, Joe slept uneasily. Even at the crew house, the one place he'd begun to feel more or less at home, it was obvious that he still remained utterly disposable.

The next day, the sophomore boat suddenly snapped back into form, handily beating all four of the other boats on its first outing. Over the next several weeks, the five potential varsity crews went at it tooth and nail, and through it all the sophomores seemed to have found themselves again. Coach Ulbrickson finally decided to list them as the first varsity boat. The following day they rowed awkwardly and lost badly. That night, writing in his logbook, Ulbrickson tore them apart: "Horrible," he wrote, "every man for himself," "no semblance of team work," "have gone to sleep entirely." Ulbrickson was beyond confused. He was starting to feel as if the sophomores might drive him nearly to madness.

He had also begun to see a great deal of unexpected talent in some of his other boats. Coach Bolles was reporting that his top freshman crew was rowing nearly as fast as Joe and his crew had the year before. They seemed to be getting better each time out. There was a curly-haired kid in the freshman boat, Don Hume, who looked particularly promising. He wasn't polished yet, but he never seemed to tire, never showed pain. He just kept going, kept driving forward, like a well-oiled locomotive. There was also a big muscular, quiet boy named Gordy Adam in the number five seat, and a kid named Johnny White in number two. White just lived and breathed rowing.

The JV boat that Bobby Moch was steering also contained a couple of promising sophomores. These boys hadn't made Joe's boat the year before, but now they were looking strong. Jim "Stub" McMillin was a six-foot-five, beanpole of a kid. Stub was big enough to provide the power that a great crew needs in the engine room, and he never seemed to believe he was beaten. Then there was a be-spectacled boy named Chuck Day, a chatterbox and a prankster. Day was the sort who tended to fight first and ask questions later. But he was also always ready with a joke.

As February gave way to March, Ulbrickson abandoned the notion of set crews. He started mixing and matching boys in different boats. First he moved Joe out of the sophomore boat. The boat slowed down. The next day Joe was back in. Ulbrickson moved Stub McMillin into the seven seat in the sophomore boat, then took him out the next day. He tried taking Joe out again, with the same weak results. He moved Shorty Hunt into Moch's JV boat.

Slowly, two favorites began to stand out. One was the original sophomore boat. The other was the JV boat with Moch, McMillin, and Day. Ulbrickson was waiting for one of them to break through, but it just wasn't happening. There were plenty of technical faults in both boats, but that was not the real problem. Ulbrickson had begun to notice that there were too many days when they rowed not as crews but as boats full of individuals. The more he scolded them for their technical issues, the more the boys seemed to sink into their own separate and sometimes defiant little worlds.

What they needed was to find something rowers call their "swing" and they were not going to get there acting like individuals. Many crews never really find their swing. It only happens when all eight oarsmen row in such perfect unison that no single action by any one of them is out of synch with those of all the others. All at once, sixteen arms must begin to pull together, sixteen knees must begin to fold and unfold in unison, eight bodies must begin to slide forward and backward, eight backs must begin to bend and straighten. Each tiny action must be mirrored exactly by each oarsman. If they can find their swing, it allows a crew to conserve energy, to move through the water as efficiently as possible, and often more rapidly than another crew that appears to be working much harder.

Joe and his crew had found their swing as freshmen the day they'd won in Poughkeepsie. Al Ulbrickson had not forgotten that. He could not, in fact, get the picture of it out of his mind. There had been something marvelous, almost magical, about how they closed out that race. He had to believe they could find it again.

Joe at Harry's new house on Lake Washington

# 15

## Battle in California

The nasty weather that had assaulted Seattle since the previous October finally broke. On April 2, a warm sun blossomed over Lake Washington. Students emerged from the mustiness of the library and the dankness of their rented rooms. At the shell house, the crew boys stripped off their jerseys and stretched out on the ramp, basking in the sun. Joe figured a day out on the water would be good for Joyce. Her hatred for the job at the judge's house was growing with each passing day. She needed a break, so they rented a canoe and Joe paddled them briskly across the Montlake Cut. He made his way lazily among the green expanse of lily pads and beaver lodges on the south side of Union Bay until he found a spot he liked. Then he let the boat drift.

Joyce reclined in the bow, trailing a hand in the water, soaking up the sun. Joe stretched out as best he could in the stern and gazed up into the blue sky. From time to time, a frog croaked and plopped into the water. Blue dragonflies hovered overhead, their wings rattling dryly. After a while, Joe took his guitar out of its battered old case and began to sing. At first he sang the songs he and Joyce had sung on the school bus back in Sequim—funny happy-go-lucky songs that made them both laugh. Then Joe slipped into soft, slow, sweet love songs, and Joyce grew quiet, watching him and listening, happy in a different, deeper way. When Joe stopped playing, they talked about what it would be like when they were married and had a home and maybe kids. They talked all afternoon, with no sense of time passing, until the chill of evening finally sent them paddling back to the university side of the bay. It was a day that both of them would remember well into old age.

The next day Joe, still feeling good after his day with Joyce, bought a little gas and drove over to the bakery where his father worked as a mechanic. He rolled the window down and waited, trying to enjoy the smell of baking bread but too nervous to really savor it. A little after noon, men dressed in white streamed out of the building and began sitting on the lawn, opening lunch boxes. Then a few men in dark coveralls emerged. Joe spotted his father immediately. At six foot two, he was easily the tallest man in the group. Joe climbed out of the car and trotted across the street.

Harry looked up, saw him coming, and froze in place, clutching his lunch box. Joe stuck out his hand and said, "Hi, Pop."

Startled, Harry said nothing but took his son's hand. It had been five and a half years since he'd seen Joe. He was no longer the scrawny kid he had left behind in Sequim. Harry had to wonder what Joe was doing there. Had his son come to confront him or forgive him?

"Hi, Joe," he said slowly. "It's swell to see you."

The two of them crossed the street and climbed into the front of Joe's car. Harry unwrapped a salami sandwich and silently offered half of it to Joe. They began to eat, and then, after a long, awkward silence, to talk. Harry spoke about the machinery and equipment in the bakery, and Joe said little at first. He wasn't much interested in the machinery, just happy to be hearing the sound of his father's big, deep, familiar voice.

When Joe finally started to talk, questions about his half siblings tumbled out: How was Harry Junior doing? How big was Mike now? How were the girls getting on? Harry assured him they were all well. There was a long pause. Joe asked if he could come by and see them. Harry looked down at his lap and said, "I don't reckon so, Joe." Deep down in Joe's gut, something surged. Anger, disappointment, resentment? He couldn't quite place the emotion, but it was old and familiar and painful.

But then, without looking up, Harry added, "Sometimes Thula and I go off on little excursions, though. Nobody home but the kids then."

In early April, the Pacific Coast Regatta was approaching. This year the Washington crews would face California on its own waters. As the day of the race grew nearer, Joe and the boys could not seem to hold on to their magic. One day they'd have it; the next day they'd lose it. They would beat the junior varsity on Monday, lose badly on Tuesday, win again on Wednesday, lose on Thursday. There was no clear favorite in the competition for the first boat, but Ulbrickson had to make a decision. Finally, he placed his faith in the sophomores and made them the 1935 first varsity crew. The local newspapers announced it to the world. The sophomores promptly lost their next head-to-head race against the JV boat.

Once again, Ulbrickson changed his mind. He declared that the two boats would race one more time, on the Oakland Estuary, a few days before the regatta. The winning boat would row as the varsity. On April 10, after the team traveled down to California, Ulbrickson staged the race. Joe and his sophomore crewmates came in almost a length behind the JV. The sophomores slumped in their shell in disbelief. The JV had won the right to row as varsity. Yet Ulbrickson still hesitated. The sophomores had come south with a new shell, and they did not like it. They had been complaining since they arrived that it just didn't swing for them. So Ulbrickson sent them out again in their old shell, the *City of Seattle*. This time they rowed beautifully and matched the JV's time.

After a team dinner at the Hotel Oakland that night, Ulbrickson dropped the bomb on the JV. He told them that he was going to race the sophomores as the varsity despite their repeated defeats. "I'm sorry," he said. "I probably shouldn't do this, but I can't help it."

The JV boys walked out of the room in a rage.

When reporters asked Ulbrickson about the series of reversals, he said simply what he believed in his heart about the sophomores. They were, he declared, "potentially the best crew I have ever coached."

Race day, April 13, was rainy, and a stiff headwind blew out of the south, up the length of the Oakland Estuary. The estuary was not a pretty place to row. Crumbling brick warehouses, oil storage tanks, rusting cranes, and gritty factories lined both sides of the waterway. The water itself was gray green and oil slicked.

Right next to Cal's shell house, a four-inch pipe discharged raw sewage directly into the estuary.

By midafternoon, nearly forty thousand spectators had assembled. They gathered under umbrellas in empty lots, on scattered docks, on warehouse rooftops, and on small craft moored along the racecourse. At the finish line, on the Fruitvale Avenue Bridge, thousands of California fans in blue and gold mingled with hundreds of Washington loyalists in purple and gold. Everyone was jostling to get a good view of the water.

The freshman race went off first, with Washington stroke Don Hume easily powering the boat to a three-length victory over Cal. The JV raced next, and with Bobby Moch calling the cadence and big Stub McMillin in the engine room, Washington dominated again, winning by a staggering eight lengths.

As Joe and the sophomore varsity paddled to their starting position, they figured they pretty much had to win now, after what the boys in the JV had just done. Once they started, Washington leapt out to an early lead. Cal raised its rate and pulled even, then moved out in front by half a length. Both boats settled in and held their positions for the next mile and a half. The blades of the two boats were dipping in and out of the water almost stroke for stroke. At the halfway point, California slowly increased its rate and stretched its lead out to a full length. George Morry, the Washington coxswain, called for more. Ever so slowly, the boys began to claw their way back, inch by inch. They whittled the lead down to a quarter of a length. Then they were bow to bow. Cal raised its stroke rate, but Washington remained steady and nosed out ahead.

The boats surged into view of the fans at the finish line, up on the bridge. California started to sprint, charging forward again, back into the lead. The Cal fans erupted in cheers. But George Morry did not panic. He resisted the temptation to call for a higher stroke rate, knowing his boys still had plenty of power.

Then, as the bridge loomed ahead, he leaned forward and called out, "Gimme ten big ones!" The Washington boys dug hard. The boat leapt forward. At the end of the ten strokes, the bows of the boats were dead even again. With the bridge and the finish line closing on them, Morry screamed again, "Gimme ten more!" Joe and Shorty and Roger and everyone with an oar in his hands threw everything they had into the last few pulls. The boats shot under the bridge side by side.

On the bridge pandemonium broke out. Someone called out that Washington won by two feet. The Washington fans roared. The loudspeaker boomed out, "Looks like California won by two feet." The Cal fans roared. Radio announcers hesitated and then beamed the news out to the nation: "California wins." The Washington fans on the bridge were furious, shouting and pointing angrily down at the water. Their boys had surged ahead at the end. Anyone could see that. The pandemonium increased. Then, suddenly, the loudspeaker crackled back to life: "The judges announce officially that Washington won by six feet."

A few days later, on April 18, the city of Seattle held a parade for the victorious Washington crews. Eighty members of the Washington Husky marching band led the procession up Second Avenue and Pike Street as confetti and scraps of paper mixed with a steady, cold rain drifting down from clouds high above. Al Ulbrickson and Tom Bolles rode with the mayor in a flower-bedecked car. Then came the main attraction—a long logging truck draped in flowers and green foliage carrying the varsity crew and their shell. The boys wore white sweaters with big purple *W*s emblazoned on them. Each held a twelve-foot-long oar upright. Joe knew Joyce was at work, so he scanned the faces in the crowd, looking for his father or his half siblings. They were nowhere to be seen.

At the Washington Athletic Club, the boys were ushered into a smoky room packed with hundreds of Seattle's leading citizens. The boys from all three boats were called up onto a stage and introduced, one at a time, each to long, sustained applause.

When it was Joe's turn, he stood for a moment looking out over the scene before him. White light poured into the room from tall windows flanked by heavy velvet curtains. Enormous crystal chandeliers hung shimmering from high, ornately plastered ceilings. Wealthy men and women sat at tables spread with gleaming silverware and platters heaped with hot food. Waiters in white coats and black bow ties scurried among the tables, carrying trays with still more food.

As Joe raised a hand to acknowledge the wave of applause, he found himself struggling desperately to keep back tears. He had never let himself dream of standing in a place like this, surrounded by people like these. He felt a sudden surge of something unfamiliar—a sense of pride that was deeper and more heartfelt than any he had ever felt before. Now it was on to the national championships again, and then, the next year, maybe even Berlin. Everything finally seemed to be turning golden.

Poughkeepsie at night

# 16
# Rage, Fear, and Uncertainty

On the first day of training for the Poughkeepsie Regatta, Ulbrickson surprised everyone by announcing that the sophomores weren't necessarily going to remain the first varsity boat. The boys in the junior varsity boat, he said, deserved a shot at a national varsity championship. Joe and the other sophomores couldn't believe it. They hadn't just beaten another crew on the estuary. They'd beaten the defending national champions. Furious, they decided to put the JV boys in their place as soon as they got out on the water.

Instead they did the opposite. Ulbrickson raced the two boats against each other again and again all through May. Occasionally the sophomores won, but usually they lost. They rowed well when left on their own, but months of taunting had gotten under their skin. Too often, the moment they got a glimpse of the older boys they fell apart completely. Ulbrickson was furious. In April he had crowed to the press that his all-sophomore crew was great—"possibly the greatest crew I have coached," he had said. Now they seemed bent on making a fool of him. At the end of May, after another impressive JV victory, Ulbrickson made another difficult decision. Washington had not won the varsity race at Poughkeepsie since 1926, when Ulbrickson himself was rowing stroke. He needed the victory and the JV boat now seemed to offer the best chance. So Ulbrickson announced that barring some kind of miracle, the older boys would race as the varsity crew for the national championship.

The trip to Poughkeepsie was not the boisterous and carefree jaunt of the year before. The weather was hot all the way across the country, the train stuffy and uncomfortable. The sophomores and the older boys tried to stay out of each other's way. Joe and Shorty Hunt and Roger Morris kept largely to themselves in one corner of a coach. There was no singing this time; Joe had left his guitar at home.

After arriving in Poughkeepsie, the Washington Husky crews visited each of their rivals' shell houses. None of the others could believe the sophomores had been demoted. At each stop Ulbrickson had to explain it all over again, to his fellow coaches. Yes, indeed—despite what had happened in California—he planned to send the older boys off in the varsity race and enter the sophomores in the junior varsity race. The coaches were shocked. So was the press. Several Seattle sportswriters had openly questioned whether he'd made the right decision. One writer pointed out that the sophomores always seemed to get stronger as their races went on, and the Poughkeepsie course would be a mile longer than the one in Oakland.

By the time they got to rowing on the Hudson River, conditions were tough out on the water. It was rainy, and a cold, stiff wind was whipping downstream. The river was a heaving mass of rollers, the water dark and oily. The conditions

After the qualifying race

were so bad that the Washington boats were the only ones out on the water. All the other crews were content to remain in the warmth of their shell houses.

The Bears from California had the warmest and coziest spot of all, a brand-spanking-new boathouse complete with clean water, hot showers, a dining room, cooking facilities, electric lights, and spacious sleeping quarters. The Washington boys were stuck in the same rickety old building as the year before, with its leaky roof and cold river-water showers. This year they'd brought their own drinking water all the way from Washington, but the sleeping arrangements were even worse than last time. They had to bunk nine to a room, instead of six.

As many as a hundred thousand people had been expected for the regatta, but by midafternoon only perhaps a third of that number had showed up. It was a miserably wet, blustery day, with rain slanting down out of dark skies in torrents. Fewer than a hundred sailboats, houseboats, and yachts had made their way to the finish line, where they lay swaying and bobbing at anchor. As race time approached, dark masses of people huddled under umbrellas made their way down the steep descent from Main Street to the water. The observation train began to fill up, though this year the open-sided cars were not as popular as the enclosed coaches.

A little before 4:00 p.m., in a driving rain, Tom Bolles's freshmen paddled upriver and took their starting position, with Columbia on one side and California on the other. The starting gun fired, and the regatta was under way before anyone realized it. Fans along the shoreline peered through a curtain of rain, struggling to distinguish one boat from another.

For thirty strokes, it was a race. Then, with Don Hume at stroke, big Gordy Adam in the middle of the boat, and the tenacious Johnny White up in seat number two all settling into their rhythms, the Washington freshmen began to pull ahead. They eased out in front of the others as if it took no effort at all. Coach Bolles became agitated, then excited, and then, finally, by all accounts, "hysterical," waving his soggy old good-luck fedora hat in the air. He believed his freshmen were an even better crew than the previous year's bunch, and they were proving him right. They slid across the line, defeating California by four lengths.

The rain had slowed a bit by 5:00 p.m., when the junior varsity race was set to go off. But it was still windy and the water was still rough. As Joe paddled upriver toward the starting line, he, like his crewmates, had a lot to think about. Cal had not sent a JV boat to Poughkeepsie, but Navy had a strong crew. The greatest danger, though, lay in his own shell. The recent defeats had shaken his self-confidence. The others boys were doubting themselves too. Everyone from Seattle to New York seemed to want to know what had happened to them since their victory in California. But neither Joe nor anybody else in the boat could begin to answer the question. As they sat at the starting line, in the *City of Seattle*, rolling with the choppy waves, waiting for the crack of the starting gun, with rainwater running down their necks and backs and dripping from their noses, the question wasn't whether they were strong or skilled enough. The real question was whether they had the maturity and discipline to keep their minds in the boat. Could they focus? Or would their anger and fear and uncertainty unhinge them?

When the gun sounded, they got away slowly and fell behind almost immediately. For half a mile, it looked as if they might, in fact, disintegrate as a crew. Then something that had been missing for a long while slowly kicked in. Realizing that they were losing, their determination took over and began to conquer their despair. They began to pull in long, sweet strokes, rowing at a composed beat of thirty-three strokes per minute. By the end of the first mile, they had found their swing and surged into the lead, quickly passing Cornell, Navy, and Syracuse. For the rest of the race, the sophomores rowed gorgeously—a long sleek line of perfection—finishing a comfortable two lengths ahead of Navy. A Seattle radio announcer was struck by how easy they had made it look. At the end of the race, he declared, the boys looked as if they could have kept on rowing right down the river all the way to New York City without breaking a sweat.

In the press section of the observation train, Al Ulbrickson watched silently. His freshmen had won. The junior varsity too. He now had a chance of doing what no coach had ever done, winning all three Poughkeepsie races in the eight-oared shells, and coming home to Seattle with a clean shot at going to Berlin. Yet he knew that Cal's varsity crew was very strong. After the loss in Oakland, Ky Ebright had switched up his varsity, moving four boys from the previous year's national championship crew back into his top boat. Ulbrickson had to wonder if Cal's losing crew in Oakland had been a trick. Maybe Ebright had been saving his best boat for Poughkeepsie.

As six o'clock and the start of the climactic race approached, the weather improved, and the crowds grew. Nobody in town that day wanted to miss out on seeing what sort of crew Ulbrickson had come up with. Everyone wanted to see the boat that was good enough to displace his talented sophomores.

Seven crews paddled to the starting line in a ghostly light mist. California had drawn lane number one, nearest the western bank of the river, where the current was least likely to affect a boat. Washington was right next door, in lane number two. Navy, Syracuse, Cornell, Columbia, and Pennsylvania stretched out across the river in lanes three through seven.

The referee called, "Ready all?" One by one, the coxswains lowered their hands. The starting gun fired. All seven boats lurched off the line together. Rowing stroke for stroke, they remained tightly bunched up for a hundred yards. Then Washington slowly edged out to a slight lead of about four feet. In the stern, Bobby Moch told his crew to settle in. At a half mile, Washington still had the lead, with Syracuse just behind them, then Navy. Cornell and California were trailing badly.

Over the next half mile, Washington expanded its lead over Syracuse, but Cornell slowly moved up on the outside. Cal still trailed the field. At a mile and a half, Washington was out in front by open water and stretching its lead. On the observation train, Cal's coach, Ky Ebright, was worried. He leaned forward, peering through a pair of binoculars, studying his boys. Washington fans on the train began hooting and hollering. Fans on the docks and yachts in Poughkeepsie began to cheer. Many of them wanted this crew to accomplish the historic feat and sweep the races, even if it was a western crew that did it.

As they crossed the two-and-a-half-mile mark, Washington's lead began to shrink. Navy and Syracuse were fading, but California and Cornell were finally starting to move up, inch by inch. Like Ebright, Al Ulbrickson was studying his boys intently through binoculars. He was still half a mile from doing what he desperately wanted to do, and he knew it. Bobby Moch was riding the stern of the Washington boat like a jockey, leaning forward into the rain, urging the boat on, screaming for them to take the stroke rate higher, then higher still. In the middle of the boat, big Stub McMillin was taking huge, powerful, smooth strokes. Up front, Chuck Day was trying to keep the boat in perfect balance stroke after stroke even as Moch kept calling for more. But they were running out of steam, and California and Cornell just kept coming.

At mile three Cornell nosed out in front. Then Cal came up to match them. Slowly, agonizingly, Washington fell into third. Over the final mile, Cal and Cornell battled for the lead, but Washington fell two lengths behind. As the leaders crossed the line, both crews thought they'd won. Minutes later the official results were announced: Ky Ebright and California had won their third straight national varsity title, by one-third of a second. And they'd done it in near record time, despite a stiff crosswind and heavy chop. The only boat ever to have turned in a faster time was Ebright's own Olympic gold medal crew of 1928. It looked more than ever as if California would be going to Berlin the following year.

The town of Grand Coulee, with B Street off to the right

# 17

# Difficult and Dangerous Work

Joe's old car labored and coughed and wheezed, crawling up the long, steep ascent to Blewett Pass, high in the Cascade Mountains. That morning, in June of 1935, he had thrown his banjo and his clothes in the backseat, said good-bye to Joyce for the summer, and driven out of Seattle, heading east, looking for work. Jobs were still scarce, but there was hope for Joe. The previous summer, President Franklin D. Roosevelt had traveled out to Washington, to a town near the Columbia River and a fifty-mile-long dry canyon called the Grand Coulee. Twenty thousand people gathered to hear him speak, among them George Pocock and his family. When President Roosevelt appeared on the platform before them, the crowd roared its welcome, and when he spoke of plans to build a massive new dam in that rough, empty country, they cheered again. The Grand Coulee Dam, he said, would bring water to arid farmland, generate electrical power, and create thousands of jobs.

Now, less than a year after Roosevelt's speech, Joe drove down from the mountains, through gently rolling jade-green wheat fields, into the rugged Washington scablands, then on to the ramshackle boomtown of Grand Coulee, perched just above the Columbia River. Thirty minutes after he stepped out of his car, he had a job. To build the foundation of the dam, hundreds of workers first had to knock away layers of loose rock from the canyon walls, to get to the older granite bedrock. Then the granite itself had to be shaped. The men who performed this work had to strap themselves into harnesses, dangle from the cliff face hundreds of feet above the river, and pound away at the rock with jackhammers. The work was difficult and dangerous, but it paid better than the other jobs at the dam. Joe signed himself up, for seventy-five cents an hour.

That evening, before his first day of work, he sat on the hood of his car, in front of the office. Down in the coulee, steam shovels and electric shovels clawed at piles of loose rock. Bulldozers pushed earth and rocks from one place to another. Tractors crawled back and forth, gouging out terraces. On the cliffs, men suspended from ropes crawled and swung from one spot to another like so many black spiders. Studying them, Joe saw that they were drilling holes in the rock faces with jackhammers. As he watched, a long, shrill whistle blew, and the jackhammer men scrambled quickly to the tops of their lines. At the base of the cliffs, hundreds of men who'd been loosening the fallen rock with picks and crowbars suddenly scurried away. The deep, hollow, concussive sound of an explosion boomed and blossomed across the canyon. A shower of rocks and boulders tumbled down onto the piles below.

Joe was not at all sure what he was getting into here. But he was flat broke again and more than a little discouraged. Not just about money but about the whole crew business. Demoted and promoted and demoted again, he'd started to think of himself as a kind of yo-yo in the hands of the coaches. And yet the notion of Olympic gold had begun to work its way into his brain. A medal would be real and solid. It would be forever. Something nobody could deny or take away. He wanted that gold medal now, and it surprised him how much it had begun to mean to him. He figured it had something to do with Thula. Or with his father. Certainly it had something to do with Joyce. He felt more and more that he had to get to Berlin to prove something to himself and to his family. To do that, he had to make the first varsity boat. And to do that, he had to pay for another year of school. That meant strapping on a harness, grabbing a jackhammer, and lowering himself over the edge of a cliff in the morning.

The jackhammer work was brutal. For eight hours a day, he dangled on a rope in the furnace-like heat of the canyon, pounding at the wall of rock in front of him. The jackhammer was heavy and seemed to have a life of its own, constantly trying to rip itself out of his grip. Rock dust, gritty and irritating, swirled around him. It got in his eyes, his mouth, and his nose. Sharp chips and shards of rock flew up and stung his face. Sweat dripped from his back and fell away into the void below. He learned to cooperate closely with the men dangling on either side of him. They worked together, keeping an eye out for rocks falling from above, dodging them when they did, calling out warnings to those below, searching for better places to find seams in the rock.

By the end of each day, he was exhausted, parched with thirst, and ravenously hungry. Three times a day, he ate in the mess hall, sitting shoulder to shoulder with men at long tables. He ate as he had back in his boyhood at the Gold and Ruby mine, tucking into mountains of food. Eggs, pancakes, bacon, and sausage at breakfast. Then sandwiches and ice cream for lunch. Finally a huge meal of red meat or chicken at dinner, topped off with slabs of pie. Joe never left a scrap on his plate or anyone else's within reach.

Each night he climbed up the hill to a place called Shack Town, where he had found a cheap room to rent in a long rickety shedlike building. The building had no indoor plumbing and only enough electricity to supply one bare lightbulb that hung overhead. Each of the gravel streets in Shack Town had a shower house, but Joe soon found that taking a shower was not a comfortable experience. Hordes of black widow spiders lurked in the rafters above the showers, and they tended to drop on the men below as soon as the water was turned on. After watching a few of his neighbors leap out of the shower yelping and batting at themselves, Joe finally took to carrying a broom into the shower each evening to clear the rafters of eight-legged invaders before he turned the water on.

For the first couple of weeks, Joe kept mostly to himself after work and dinner, sitting in the dark, playing his banjo. Then he discovered that there were two boys from the Washington shell house working at the dam as well. He didn't know either of them very well, but that was about to change. Johnny White had sat in the number two seat in Coach Bolles's outstanding freshman boat. He was an inch shorter than Joe, and more slightly built, with all-American good looks. He was also nearly as poor as Joe Rantz. He graduated from high school at sixteen, then spent the next two years working in a shipyard and a sawmill, saving cash and building brawn. Now he'd arrived at Grand Coulee looking to make more money and build more muscle.

The other Washington boy at Grand Coulee was Chuck Day. He was pure muscle, broad in the shoulders, and his eyes could be cheerful one moment, flashing with rage the next. He wore glasses but managed to look tough doing it, and despite Ulbrickson's rules, he almost always had a cigarette dangling from his lip. The previous year he had rowed in Bobby Moch's boat. He and Joe had hardly ever exchanged two words, at least not civil words.

Now, though, the three boys fell into an easy and comfortable friendship. Without a word, they put aside the rivalries of the shell house, forgot about the insults. After their long, crushingly hard workweeks, they gathered on Saturday afternoons to escape the heat and watch movies at the Grand Coulee Theater. At night they wandered B Street, a three-block stretch of dirt and gravel lined on either side with card rooms and bars and pool halls and fleabag hotels and a Chinese restaurant, the Woo Dip Kitchen. Jazz and country music poured out of the bars and dance halls. The boys took it all in with wide eyes. None of them had ever seen anything quite like it, and they weren't sure how to behave in this new world. They remembered Al Ulbrickson's rules—no smoking, no drinking, no cussing—but there were many temptations. They drank some beer and played some pool and sang along with ragtag cowboy bands late into the night.

When they wanted to escape the noise of B Street, the boys sometimes traveled down the coulee to swim in Soap Lake. For the most part, though, they stayed in Grand Coulee, where they could toss a football around, hurl rocks off the edges of the cliffs, or sit around a campfire at night telling ghost stories as coyotes yelped in the distance. They were happy, free, and easy, cut loose in the wide expanse of the western desert, ignoring for now the contest that they all knew lay ahead the following year.

Bobby Moch

# 18

## The Parts That Really Matter

In mid-September, Joe returned from Grand Coulee with enough money to make it through another year. Joyce had abruptly left her job that summer, after the judge had taken an inappropriate interest in her and chased her around the dining table one afternoon. Luckily she found work with another family nearby. The new job started off on an uncertain note. On the first evening, the lady of the house, Mrs. Tellwright, asked her to make a difficult dish, duck *à l'orange*, for dinner. Joyce was horrified. She knew what a duck was and what an orange was but nothing about how to bring them together in a recipe. Mrs. Tellwright found Joyce's effort to be pretty much inedible. Instead of firing her though, she quietly pulled Joyce aside and suggested that the two of them take cooking classes together. They did, and that turned out to be the beginning of a long and happy friendship.

Joe resumed visiting his father at the bakery, and Harry mentioned again that he and Thula sometimes took trips by themselves, which meant Joe could visit his half siblings without worrying about Thula throwing him out of the house. The first time he and Joyce visited, though, they were shocked. They found that his father and Thula had been gone for three straight days, and the kids were hungry, almost entirely out of food. Harry Junior, the oldest at thirteen, said that his parents had packed a pressure cooker full of stewed beef, potatoes, and vegetables, taken a loaf of bread and some canned goods, and gone to Medical Lake in eastern Washington. He didn't know when they might return. Joe and Joyce took the kids out for ice cream, then bought some basic provisions before dropping them back home. By the next day, when Joe drove by to check, Harry and Thula had returned. But he could not figure out what they'd been thinking.

Apparently this had been going on all summer long. Thula had begun to pursue her dream of becoming a violinist. That summer, she'd had an audition with a major violinist in Los Angeles, and a local radio station had aired a series of her live performances. Now she was bent on getting out of the house, celebrating, and enjoying her success.

Joe headed back to the shell house to get in shape for what was to come. Johnny White and Chuck Day showed up too, dusty and tanned from Grand Coulee. Coach Ulbrickson was back as well, and his desire for Olympic gold had only grown stronger over the summer. He told his wife in private that if he didn't fetch gold in Berlin in 1936, he planned to quit coaching. To pull it off, though, he knew he had to find nine young men of exceptional strength, grace, endurance, and most of all mental toughness. They would have to row almost flawlessly in long races and short, under all kinds of conditions. They would have to live well together in close quarters for weeks at a time. They would have to perform on the most prominent stage in the sport, in full view of the whole world. He believed he had such boys somewhere at the shell house, but he had not identified them yet. To find that ideal crew, Ulbrickson had begun to turn to George Pocock for advice.

At some point that fall, as he talked to Pocock, the subject of Joe Rantz came up. Ulbrickson had been studying Joe for a year now, ever since Tom Bolles had told him about the boy. Since then, Ulbrickson had tried everything. He'd scolded Joe, encouraged him, demoted him, promoted him. But he wasn't any closer to understanding the mystery of Joe Rantz. There were days when he rowed like quicksilver, so smooth and fluid and powerful that he seemed a part of the boat and his oar and the water all at once. But there were other days when he was downright lousy, when he seemed to row as if his mind was somewhere else, lost in his own little world. Now Ulbrickson asked Pocock to take a look at the boy. He wanted Pocock to talk to him, to try to figure him out, and, if possible, to fix him.

On a bright, crisp September morning, as Pocock started up the steps to his loft in the shell house, he noticed Joe doing sit-ups on a bench at the back of the room. He motioned Joe to come over, said he'd noticed him peering up into the workshop occasionally. He asked if he'd like to look around. Joe was thrilled. Like Pocock, he loved working with wood, and he wanted desperately to see the shop. He all but bounded up the stairs.

The loft was bright and airy, with morning light pouring in from two large windows in the back wall. The air was thick with the sweet-sharp scent of marine varnish. Drifts of sawdust and curls of wood shavings lay on the floor. An eight-oared shell was under construction in the center of the room.

Pocock started off by explaining the various tools he used. He showed Joe his wood planes, their wooden handles burnished by decades of use, their blades so sharp and precise they could shave off curls of wood as thin and transparent as tissue paper. He handed him tools he'd brought over from England, some of which were a century old. He guided Joe to a lumber rack and pulled out samples of soft, malleable sugar pine, hard yellow spruce, fragrant cedar, and clear white ash.

Joe grew mesmerized. It wasn't just what the Englishman was saying, it was the way he talked about the wood, as if it was holy and sacred. He told of how the trees had grown in all sorts of conditions, endured lightning strikes and wind-storms and infestations. Pocock said the wood taught us about survival, about overcoming difficulty, but it also taught us about the reason for surviving in the first place. Something about infinite beauty, about things larger and greater than ourselves.

"Sure, I can make a boat," he said, and then added, quoting the poet Joyce Kilmer, "'but only God can make a tree.'"

Pocock pulled out a thin sheet of cedar, one that had been milled down to three-eighths of an inch. The sheet would form the skin of a shell. Pocock flexed the wood and had Joe do the same. He talked about the underlying strength of the individual fibers in the wood. He said those separate fibers, knitted together in the wood, gave cedar its ability to bounce back and resume its shape or take on a new one. The ability to yield, to bend, to give way, Pocock said, was sometimes a source of strength in men as well as in wood.

Pocock stepped back and studied the shell he was building. To build a boat, he told Joe, you had to give yourself up to it spiritually. You had to surrender yourself absolutely to your work, leave a part of your heart in it. He turned to Joe. "Rowing," he said, "is like that. And a lot of life is like that too, the parts that really matter anyway. Do you know what I mean, Joe?"

Joe nodded, but he was not at all certain that he did. He went back downstairs and resumed his sit-ups, trying to work it out.

Varsity practice did not begin officially until October 21. In the meantime, Joe and Joyce paddled canoes around the bay, window-shopped downtown, went to the movies, and stopped by his father's house whenever Harry and Thula were away. When they could, they'd take Joe's half siblings out for quick picnics on Green Lake, then rush the kids back home before Harry and Thula returned.

Joe spent much of his free time at the shell house, exercising and tossing a football around with Johnny White, Chuck Day, Roger Morris, and Shorty Hunt. He found another friend in Stub McMillin, the gangly number five man from the previous year's JV boat. Joe would often linger at the shell house late into the evening, and one night he came out of the steam room to find Stub pushing a broom. When Joe realized Stub was working as the shell house janitor, he sauntered over and stuck out his hand. As they talked, Joe confided what he had long kept secret from the other boys. He told Stub that he was now a janitor too, working a late-night shift at the YMCA.

When varsity practice began, the previous season's rivalries and hard feelings and insecurities erupted again. There was no fiery speech from Coach Ulbrickson this time. There was no need for it. Everyone knew exactly what the stakes were this year. Ulbrickson gathered all the boys on the ramp, straightened his tie, and announced that there would be no set boats. He was going to mix and match the boys until he found the ideal crew. Until then it was going to be every man for himself.

For the next few weeks, Joe bumped back and forth between the third and fourth boats. He was rowing hard, but his spirits were starting to flag. He missed the camaraderie that had grown among his classmates after two years of rowing together. He missed Shorty Hunt sitting behind him, whispering, "Don't worry, Joe. I've got your back," whenever Ulbrickson yelled at him. He missed gruff Roger Morris, who rarely said a word but was always there for him. Joe hadn't really thought before about how much it mattered to him that those two fellows were in the boat with him. But it turned out that it did matter, a lot.

He had the same feeling every time he watched his Grand Coulee buddy Johnny White sweep by him in another boat, part of something else now, part of a crew of boys dead set on defeating him. When he was abandoned in Sequim, he promised himself he'd never depend on anyone else, not even on Joyce, for his happiness or his sense of who he was. Now he began to see that he'd allowed himself to do exactly that, with the usual painful results. He hadn't expected it. He hadn't prepared for it. And now the ground seemed to be shifting under him in an unpredictable way.

Then, just a few days into the season, the ground shifted again. Joe learned that Thula was dead, killed by an infection. He was numb. He didn't know what to think or to feel. Although she'd abandoned him and turned him away, Thula had been the closest thing to a mother that he had known since he was three. There had been at least some good times back in Spokane when they had all sat together on the big swing in the backyard. Over the years he had wondered what he might have done to make things better between them. Now he would never know. Mostly, though, he worried about how his father, and even more his half siblings, would cope with the change.

The next morning Joe went by his father's house. He found his father and the kids sitting at a picnic table on a soggy lawn. They talked for a while about Thula's life. Joe told his father how sorry he was.

Finally Harry turned abruptly to Joe and said, "Son, I've got a plan. I'm going to build a house where we can all live together. As soon as it's done, I want you to come home."

Joe sat at the table staring at his father. He did not know what to make of the proposal. He did not know if he could trust the man. He stammered out a vague answer. They talked some more about Thula. Joe told the kids that he would be coming by more often to keep them company from now on. But he drove back to the YMCA that night not sure what to do. Slowly his confusion turned to anger, which gave way again to confusion and then anger again, all of it washing over him in waves.

THE 1936 VARSITY CREW

Left to right: Don Hume, Joe Rantz, Shorty Hunt, Stub McMillin, Johnny White, Gordy Adam, Chuck Day, Roger Morris. Kneeling: Bobby Moch

# 19

# A Truth to Come to Terms With

The rest of the fall season was grueling, as the boys rowed and raced in weather that had again turned unusually cold and stormy. Joe's boat often finished third. He was struggling with his emotions, especially since Thula had died and his father had invited him to move home. Then he got a letter from Sequim. Charlie McDonald was dead too, killed in an automobile crash. Charlie had been an adviser and a teacher to Joe, the one adult who had stood by him when no one else had. Now he was gone, and Joe found himself unable to focus. His mind was almost never in the boat, and it showed in his rowing. But it didn't seem to matter. As far as Joe could tell, no one in the coach's motorboat was even paying attention to him anymore.

But in fact someone was watching him very closely. Joe had noticed that Pocock was riding along in the motorboat frequently these days, but he hadn't noticed where Pocock had been training his binoculars.

When the boys returned to the shell house after Christmas break, Ulbrickson warned them that they "must be ready to take part in Washington's greatest and most grueling crew season." After months of talking about the Olympic year, it was finally here. On the first Monday of the new season, Joe was surprised to find his name listed among those in the number one varsity boat. He couldn't fathom why he had suddenly been promoted. As it turned out, it wasn't really much of a promotion. Ulbrickson planned to spend the first few weeks working on technique and fundamentals, and he believed the boys would be more receptive if they were rowing with familiar crewmates. So Joe was back with the boys from freshman year, including Shorty Hunt and Roger Morris.

Through January and into February, they rowed six days a week. They worked on individual weaknesses. When it wasn't snowing, it was clear, bitter cold, and windy. Icicles dangled from the bow of the boat. They rowed anyway, with white knuckles and chattering teeth, some of them dressed in ragged sweat suits, some in shorts and stocking caps. Occasionally they staged short races against each other, and Joe's boat kept coming in third. The third boat kept coming in first.

In general Ulbrickson was pleased. By late February he was starting to form some solid ideas about what his Olympic boat would look like. One choice was obvious. No matter what, Bobby Moch, the clever, fiery coxswain from the previous year's JV crew, was going to be sitting in the stern. At five foot seven and 119 pounds, he was almost the perfect size for a coxswain. Pocock, in fact, designed his shells to perform best with a 120-pound coxswain.

Despite his small frame, a coxswain had to be strong enough to steer the boat. He had to know enough about the oarsmen inside, their individual strengths and weaknesses, to get the most out of each rower at any given moment. And he had to have the force of character to inspire exhausted rowers to try harder, even when all seemed lost. Bobby Moch had proven he could do all of this the previous year. He had a deep baritone voice that was surprising in a man so small, and he bellowed out commands with absolute authority. Most important, he was smart and he knew how to use his smarts.

Joe's situation, on the other hand, was only getting worse. In late February he was dropped to the number two boat. On February 20, rowing hard and in a heavy snow and a steady east wind, the first two boats came in about even. Joe's hopes rose. But a week later Ulbrickson moved him down to the number three boat.

One stormy afternoon in early March, after practice, George Pocock tapped Joe on the shoulder and asked him to come up into the loft again. Upstairs, Pocock leaned over one side of a new shell and began to apply varnish to its upturned hull. Joe pulled a sawhorse to the other side and sat down on it, facing the older man.

Pocock began by saying he'd been closely watching Joe row for a while now, that he was a fine oarsman. He'd noted a few technical faults, but that wasn't what he wanted to talk about. He said that there were times when Joe seemed to think he was the only one in the boat. He rowed as if it was up to him to row the boat across the finish line all by himself. When a man rowed like that, Pocock said, he was bound to attack the water rather than to work with it. Worse, he would not be able to let his crew help him row.

The Englishman suggested that Joe think of a well-rowed race as a symphony, and himself as just one player in the orchestra. If one fellow in the orchestra was playing out of tune, or playing at a different tempo, the whole piece would naturally be ruined. That's the way it was with rowing. What mattered more than how hard a man rowed was how well everything he did in the boat harmonized with what the other fellows were doing. And a man couldn't harmonize with his crewmates unless he opened his heart to them. He had to care about everyone on his crew. He had to give himself up to the rowing, but he had to do even more. He had to give himself up to his crewmates too. "If you don't like some fellow in the boat, Joe, you have to learn to like him," Pocock said. "It has to matter to you whether he wins the race, not just whether you do."

Pocock paused and looked up. "Joe, when you really start trusting those other boys," Pocock said, "you will feel a power at work within you that is far beyond anything you've ever imagined. Sometimes, you will feel as if you have rowed right off the planet and are rowing among the stars."

The next day was a Sunday, and Joe took Joyce and drove over to a lot on Lake Washington where his father was building his new house. The land was right next to his brother Fred's house, and for the past few weekends Joe had been helping his father work. The basement was nearly complete, and with the upstairs portion under way, Harry had moved the kids in downstairs. The basement was more like a cave than a house, but Harry had lugged in a woodstove, and it was warm and dry inside.

Joe and Joyce with Joe's half-siblings

As Joe worked with his father, hauling lumber down from the road in a driving rain, Joyce entertained the kids, playing card games and making fudge and cocoa on the stove. Playing mother to Thula's children was natural to Joyce. The children were grief-stricken, and Harry's full-time work on the house prevented him from giving them the attention they needed. Every instinct Joyce had led her to sweep them into her arms and care for them. But her feelings about Harry were different. Even though he treated Joyce pleasantly, inside she still seethed with resentment toward him. She could not forgive him for his failure to stand behind Joe for all those years.

By late afternoon, after they had moved all the lumber into position, Joe stood outside on the dock by himself, staring out at the lake. The finish line for the Pacific Coast Regatta in April was a little less than a mile up the lake from there. He wondered if he would be in the varsity boat when it passed by this dock. A gust of wind struck him. Rain poured down his face. He stared at the water, pondering what Pocock had told him the day before.

Joe had spent the last six years making his own way in the world. Nothing was more frightening than allowing himself to depend on others. People let you down. People left you behind. Depending on people and trusting them got you hurt. But trust seemed to be at the heart of what Pocock was asking. Harmonize with the other fellows, he said. There was a kind of absolute truth in that. It was something Joe couldn't deny. He had to come to terms with it.

He stood on the dock for a long time, gazing at the lake, oblivious to the rain. Then he turned and peered back at the house. Inside, the kids and Joyce and his father were all under one roof, sitting in front of the fire, waiting for him to come in. When he returned to the warm cave, he toweled dry, unpacked his banjo, and gathered the kids around him. He tuned the banjo carefully. Then he cleared his throat, cracked open a big white smile and began to play and sing. One by one, the kids, then his father, and finally Joyce began to join in, singing along with him.

By March 19, Ulbrickson figured he had found his best bet for an Olympic boat. He still had it pegged as the second boat on his chalkboard, but the boys in it were beginning to edge the first boat consistently. Bobby Moch was riding coxswain. Roger Morris was in the bow, followed by Chuck Day and Gordy Adam.

In the engine room, Ulbrickson had placed Johnny White at number four, Stub McMillin in the five seat, and Shorty Hunt at number six. Merton Hatch, another of Tom Bolles's former freshmen, sat in the seven seat. The star of last year's freshman crew, Don Hume, was the stroke oar.

Joe was in the third boat. And it looked as if he'd be staying there, and staying home, not rowing in the Cal race or beyond. But then, on March 21, he walked into the shell house and found his name on the chalkboard, sitting at seat number seven in boat number two, right between Shorty Hunt and Don Hume. He couldn't believe it. He didn't know if Pocock had talked to Ulbrickson or if Merton Hatch had simply messed up in some terrible way. Whatever the reason, he had his chance. He knew what he had to do.

From the moment he stepped into the shell that afternoon, he felt at home. He liked these boys. He didn't know Gordy Adam and Don Hume well, but both made a point of welcoming him aboard. His oldest, most reliable shell house friend, Roger Morris, sitting up front in the bow, gave him a wave and shouted, "Hey, Joe, I see you finally found the right boat!" His buddies from Grand Coulee—Chuck Day and Johnny White—were sitting up near the front too. When he saw Joe, Stub McMillin, his face alight, said, "Okay, this boat is going to fly now, boys." Shorty Hunt slapped him on the back and whispered, "Got your back, Joe."

# 20
## Finding Their Swing

On that first day out with the new crew, Joe rowed as he had never been able to row before. He rowed as Pocock had told him to row, giving himself up to the crew's effort entirely, merging with it, becoming one with it. He followed Hume's stroke flawlessly, sending it back to Shorty behind him in one continuous flow. It felt to Joe like a transformation, as if some kind of magic had come over him. As he climbed out of the boat, he realized that he didn't need to struggle to give himself up to the rhythm of the boat, as Pocock had urged him to do. With this bunch of boys, he did not even have to try. He just trusted them. In the end, it was that simple.

Over the next few days, the boat began to fly, just as Stub said it would. Racing the other crews, the boat won by an astonishing seven lengths one day, three lengths another day. They won sprints. They won in wind. They won in snow. And on March 28, Ulbrickson officially declared that they were the new varsity boat. If he was going to get to the Olympics, this was the crew that was going to take him there.

That afternoon George Pocock personally christened the new shell in which the boys would row. As Joe and his crewmates held it aloft, Pocock poured a jarful of mysterious fluid over its bow and pronounced, "I christen this boat *Husky Clipper*. May it have success in all the waters it speeds over. Especially in Berlin." As the boys began to carry the boat down the ramp to the water, some of them crinkled their noses, trying to make out the odd scent of the fluid on the bow. Pocock chuckled and grinned. "Sauerkraut juice," he said. "To get it used to Germany."

Two weeks before the Pacific Coast Regatta, Ulbrickson held one final three-mile time trial. The course record was then 16:33.4, but Joe and his crewmates finished it faster, at 16:20, and they did it sitting upright at the end of the race, breathing easy, feeling good. Every time they climbed into the *Husky Clipper* together, they just seemed to get better.

There was a straightforward reason for what was happening. The boys in the *Husky Clipper* were all tough, they were all skilled, they were all fiercely determined, but they were also all good-hearted. Every one of them had come from humble origins or had been humbled by the hard demands of rowing. Life, and the challenges they had faced together, had also taught them humility—that there limits to their individual powers. They had learned that there were things they could do far better together than alone. They were starting to row now for one another, not just themselves, and it made all the difference.

Ky Ebright and the boys from Cal arrived in Seattle on April 14. The next day, when they showed up to row, the sun was out in full force, and the water was glass smooth. As they carried their shells down the ramp to the water, the national champion Cal boys were an intimidating sight. They had been rowing well under the California sun and they were tanned and fit. A week earlier they had rowed a three-mile time trial in 16:15, a good five seconds better than Ulbrickson's crew. But Ebright knew to take the Washington boys seriously. That first day, he jumped into the coxswain's seat of his varsity boat, a Pocock-crafted shell called the *California Clipper*, and barked commands himself during an eight-mile practice row.

On race day, Saturday, April 18, the skies were flawlessly blue. The weather was warm. A ferry packed with students and the school's marching band left the dock in the early afternoon. A navy cruiser and nearly four hundred other vessels flying purple and gold pennants gathered near the finish line. On the dock at Fred's house, right next to Harry's new home, Joyce and the kids and Harry sat eating peanuts and tossing the shells into the lake. By 2:15 p.m., when an observation train rolled into place, the largest crowd ever to witness a crew race in the Northwest had assembled along the racecourse.

The Washington freshmen did not disappoint, setting a new course record and winning by four and a half lengths. In the next race, Washington's JV boat took the lead easily at the start and crossed the line almost six lengths ahead of California, again setting a new course record. At 4:15 p.m., the two varsity crews paddled out to the starting line. A tailwind had stiffened, piling rough water into heaps of whitecaps at the north end of the lake. So far, all the boats on the course that day had broken course records, even the losing crews. The bodies of the oarsmen were catching the wind, acting as sails, hurrying the shells down the course.

At the starting line, the *Husky Clipper* bobbed in the swells. Roger Morris and Gordy Adam, up front, kept the bow of the boat pointed due north. Bobby Moch lowered his hand to indicate his crew was ready to row. Over in the Cal boat, the coxswain did the same. The starter shouted, "Row!" and both boats bolted off the line.

The big Cal stroke, Gene Berkenkamp, who had mowed Washington down in two races the previous year, quickly powered his crew to a short lead. For three-quarters of a mile, the two crews rowed at the same speed, both furiously digging at the choppy water. Don Hume was matching Berkenkamp's stroke rate but making no progress in overtaking him. Then Bobby Moch had a daring idea. Cal was ahead, and rowing hard, but he told Hume to *lower* the stroke count. Hume dropped it to twenty-nine. Almost immediately the boys found their swing. Don Hume set the model, taking huge, smooth, deep pulls. Joe and the rest of the boys fell in behind him. Very slowly, seat by seat, the *Husky Clipper* began to regain water on the *California Clipper*. By the one-mile mark, the two boats were even.

The Cal coxswain called out, "Give me ten big ones!" Bobby Moch hunched down in the stern, looked Don Hume in the eyes, and growled at him to keep it steady at twenty-nine. With the wind in their faces, pushing them along, both crews were flying down the course now. Spray was breaking over the bow of their shells as they skipped from wave to wave. Cal was rowing at thirty-one strokes per minute, but even with its slower rate Washington continued to inch ahead.

The Cal coxswain called for another big ten, but Bobby Moch held steady, and Washington maintained its small lead.

In Washington's number seven seat, Joe realized he was nearing his father's house. He was tempted to sneak a peek over his shoulder, but he didn't. He kept his mind in the boat. Washington moved out to a three-quarter-length lead. The Cal coxswain called on his boys to give him more. They raised their stroke rate to thirty-five, then thirty-six. Moch continued to hold steady at twenty-nine. Finally, with a half mile to go, Moch bellowed at Hume to pick up Washington's rate. The *Husky Clipper* surged forward, and in the last half mile they accelerated in a way that no shell had ever accelerated on Lake Washington. As they flew down the last few hundred yards, the boys rocked back and forth, perfectly in synch. Hundreds of boat whistles shrieked. The locomotive on the observation train wailed. Students on the ferry screamed. And a long, sustained roar went up from the tens of thousands standing along the beach as the *Husky Clipper* crossed the line three lengths ahead of California, beating the course record by 37 seconds.

As the crowds around him cheered, Al Ulbrickson sat quietly in his boat at the finish line, listening to the band play the school's fight song. His boys had beaten a very good California crew, the defending national champions. They had rowed better than ever. They were truly an out-of-the-ordinary group, but it was too early to see whether the magic would hold. Two years running now, his varsity had beaten Ebright's in the Pacific Coast Regatta, only to lose at the national championships in Poughkeepsie. Who was to say that this bunch wouldn't do the same?

# 21

# Save, Save, Save

Following the victory, Ulbrickson gave the boys two weeks off. When they returned to the shell house on May 4, they rowed raggedly for the first few days back on the water, until they found their swing again. But find it they did, and they promptly began to power past the other shells. On or off the water, they were almost always together now. They ate together, studied together, and played together. On weekend evenings they gathered around the old upright piano in the parlor of the Varsity Boat Club and sang for hours. Don Hume tore through jazz tunes, show tunes, blues, and ragtime. Sometimes Roger Morris played saxophone and Johnny White played along on his violin. And almost always Joe got out his banjo or his guitar and joined in as well. Nobody laughed at him anymore; nobody dreamed of laughing at him.

By the end of May, the boys were again turning in phenomenal times on the water. But their success in Seattle didn't guarantee victory in Poughkeepsie. The regatta on the Hudson would be a four-mile race, not three, and the California boys had proven time again that they were masters at the longer distance. On June 6, Ulbrickson took the varsity and JV out for one final four-mile trial before leaving for Poughkeepsie. He told Bobby Moch to hold the varsity back behind the JV boat for the first two miles. But as they moved down the lake, rowing at a leisurely stroke rate of twenty-six, the varsity could not manage to stay behind. They kept edging out in front simply on the power of their long, slow strokes. When Moch finally turned them loose in the final mile, they exploded into a seven-length lead, and they were still pulling away as they crossed the finish line.

Four days later, the boys arrived at Seattle's railroad station, led by a police escort with sirens wailing and red lights flashing. In the station the marching band was already playing fight songs. The crowd was packed with cheerleaders, journalists, parents, cousins, next-door neighbors, and utter strangers. The boys had not just packed for New York. They had packed as if they had already made the Olympics and were heading for Berlin. Some of them were even making plans to tour Europe after the games, although none of them were sure where they'd get the money for that. Johnny White had a grand total of fourteen dollars in his pocket. Bobby Moch was hoping to visit his relatives in Switzerland and Alsace-Lorraine. At first, his father, Gaston, hesitated to give his son their addresses. But he agreed to send them later, if the crew really went to Europe.

The boys climbed aboard, and as the train coughed, lurched, and began to pull away, they hung from the windows shouting farewells: "Good-bye, Mom!" "I'll write from Berlin." Joe hung out a window as well, searching. Then, in a far corner, he found her. Joyce was standing with his father and the kids, jumping up and down, holding a sign high over her head. In the middle of the sign she had painted a large green four-leaf clover.

The Washington boys arrived in Poughkeepsie early in the morning on June 14, in the midst of a summer thunderstorm. They were not using the rickety old shack for a boathouse this year. They moved into Cornell's former boathouse, right next to California's. The new quarters had been provided by the regatta authorities as a result of Washington's newfound respect in the East. It had hot showers, exercise facilities, electricity, and extra-long beds. And the roof didn't leak.

By the time they had finished settling in, they could smell food cooking. Led by their noses, and by Joe Rantz's nose in particular, they quickly discovered the best feature of the new place. There was a cookhouse on the beach, just twenty-five feet from their front door. An African American woman named Evanda May Calimar was in charge, and she was an awe-inspiring cook. The boys had heaps of fried chicken for lunch, and they were in heaven. Nobody appreciated it more than Joe, who went back for seconds and then thirds. Seattle's *Post-Intelligencer* newspaper published a story on their first meal, with a picture of Joe captioned "Joe Rantz, The Eating Champion."

Pocock visited the California boathouse to check on the shell he'd built them, but the Washington boys declined to speak to their rivals. On the dock they shared, the two crews passed each other silently, with eyes averted, like dogs circling before a fight. And although a fight on land was possible, a battle on the water was a near certainty. During the next few days, word leaked out that

Cal had turned in a blazing time of 19:31 over four miles. After Washington held its own time trial, Ulbrickson announced that their time was slower, a fraction of a second over 19:39. But Ulbrickson may have been trying to deceive Ky Ebright. Johnny White recorded the boys' true time in his journal that night: 19:25. The next day, though, rumors began to circulate that California had held yet another time trial, and turned in a phenomenal time of 18:46.

But Ulbrickson remained unruffled. He was not going to schedule another trial. He wanted well-rested boys in the race. He told his boys to relax. There would be only light workouts until race day, and that was fine with the boys. They already knew something that nobody else knew, not even their coach.

Late on the night of their final time trial, after the wind had died down and the waters had calmed, they had begun to row back up the river, in the dark, side by side with the freshman and JV boats. It was a moonless night. The water was ink black. Bobby Moch set the boys to rowing at a leisurely twenty-two or twenty-three. Joe and his crewmates chatted softly with the boys in the other two boats. But they soon found that they had pulled ahead without meaning to, just rowing soft and steady. Soon, in fact, they had pulled so far ahead that they could not even hear the boys talking in the other boats. And then, one by one, they realized they couldn't hear anything at all except for the gentle murmur of their blades dipping into and out of the water. They were rowing in utter darkness now. They were alone together in a realm of silence and darkness. They were rowing perfectly, fluidly, mindlessly. They were rowing in perfect unity as if on another plane, among the stars, just as Pocock had said. And it was beautiful.

By the morning of the championship regatta, the consensus in the eastern newspapers was that California and Cornell were the boats to beat in the varsity race. People crowded onto ferries, boats, and the observation train. As many as ninety thousand fans lined both sides of the Hudson River. As the starting time approached, the breeze died. The water was placid, smooth and glassy, tinged with bronze in the late afternoon light.

The freshmen came through again for Tom Bolles. He was wearing his lucky fedora, but he didn't need it, as his boys gradually overpowered Navy, then beat Cal by a boat length. An hour later, Washington's JV crossed the line three lengths ahead of Navy, still pulling away at the head of a long, strung-out parade of boats far to their rear. Even as the last boats crossed the line and the cheering began to die down, a murmur began to ripple through the crowd along the shore. Washington, for the second time in two years, now stood again on the brink of sweeping the regatta. California, on the other hand, could become only the second school ever to win the varsity race four years in a row. But anything was possible. Cornell looked as if they could finally win this year. Or maybe Navy.

As the observation train drew back upriver again for the start, the atmosphere grew electric. The crowd began to buzz. Boat whistles shrilled. Fans draped arms over one another's shoulders and sang college fight songs. On the train, in a car packed full of Washington coaches, alumni, and sportswriters, George Pocock and Tom Bolles paced up and down the aisle. Al Ulbrickson sat alone in silence, looking out from under the brim of his white cloth cap toward the spot where Joe and the boys sat in their shell, waiting. Washington had drawn the worst lane, number seven, far out in the middle of the river, where any hint of wind or current would be strongest. California had drawn the most protected lane, number one.

At 8:00 p.m., the starter called out, "Are you ready?"

The starting gun popped, and for five full strokes, all seven boats stayed even. Then Washington suddenly eased up. The other boats surged out in front of them. That was okay with Bobby Moch. That was just what he wanted. Prior to the race, Ulbrickson had explained that he had a new plan for his coxswain to follow. He wanted the boys to stay at a low, easy stroke rate, no matter what the other boats were doing. If they fell more than two boat lengths behind, he told Moch he should pick up the pace, but otherwise, he wanted them to hold off until the halfway point, then start to raise the rate and pass the leaders at the end. Now, as Moch settled his crew in, rowing at a steady twenty-eight, he began to chant their newest rowing mantra in time with the stroke—"Save, save, save"— reminding them to conserve their power.

After half a mile, Washington was in last place, almost five lengths behind the leaders. A mile into the race, Navy and Penn were in the lead, with California and Columbia close behind. Washington passed Syracuse, but remained four lengths back. On the train, Al Ulbrickson was still silent and calm, slowly chewing a stick of gum. Soon, he figured, Bobby Moch would make his move, just as they'd planned.

At two miles Penn had begun to fade, falling behind Columbia. Cal and Navy were battling for the lead. Washington was in fifth place, but Bobby Moch still hadn't altered the beat at all. Ulbrickson began to grow uneasy. He had told Moch not to let the leaders get more than two lengths ahead. Now the boys were twice that far behind. And Moch was supposed to have started moving by now.

But out on the water, Bobby Moch told Don Hume, "Take your time. We can catch those boys anytime we want."

As they passed the two-and-a-half-mile mark, Ulbrickson had begun to slump in his seat. He stopped chewing his gum. What on earth was Moch doing? Why in God's name didn't he turn them loose? Tom Bolles and George Pocock sat down, looking morose. It was starting to look like a case of suicide.

In the boat Bobby Moch took a long look at the four lengths between his bow and California's stern, and hollered to the boys facing him, "Okay, you lugs! We're one length behind."

A roar went up as the crowds near the finish line began to see the leaders. Navy was neck and neck with Cal, and the two of them seemed to be running away with it. With a mile to go, Washington was still nearly three lengths back. The boys were rowing as if in a kind of trance now. There was little sound out in the middle of the river, except for Moch's chanting, the rattle of oars in oarlocks, their own deep rhythmic breathing, and their pulses pounding in their ears. There was almost no pain. In the number five seat, Stub McMillin realized with astonishment that he was still breathing easy, through his nose. On the train, Ulbrickson muttered, "They're overplaying their hand. We'll be lucky to finish third." His face had gone white.

Then, suddenly, Bobby Moch leaned into Don Hume's face and bellowed, "Give me ten hard ones for Ulbrickson!" Eight long spruce oars bowed in the water ten times. Then Moch bellowed again, "Give me ten more for Pocock!" Another ten enormous strokes. Then another lie: "Here's California! We're on them! Ten more big ones for Mom and Dad!" Very slowly the *Husky Clipper* slipped past Columbia and began to creep up on Navy in second.

On the train, someone called out, "Look at Washington! Look at Washington! Here comes Washington!" All eyes shifted from the leaders to the eight white blades barely visible out in the middle of the river. Another roar rose from the crowd. It seemed impossible for Washington to close the gap. They were a half mile from the finish and still two lengths back.

In the boat Moch barked, "Okay! Now! Now! Now!" Don Hume took the stroke up to thirty-five, then to thirty-six, then to thirty-seven. On the starboard side, Joe Rantz fell in behind him, just as smooth as silk. The boat began to swing. The bow began to rise out of the water. Washington slid past the Navy oarsmen as if their shell were pinned to the water.

Cal's coxswain glanced over his shoulder. For the first time since he'd left it behind at the finish line he saw the Washington boat sweeping up from behind him. He bellowed at his crew to pick it up. Moch hollered at Hume to take the Washington rate up another notch. The two boats careened into the last five hundred yards, storming down the corridor of open water between the spectators' boats. With the finish line looming ahead, Bobby Moch screamed something nobody could understand. Johnny White, in the number four seat, suddenly had the sensation that they were flying. Shorty Hunt still hadn't seen the California boat fall into his field of view. He kept his eyes locked on the back of Joe Rantz's neck and pulled with his whole heart. Joe had boiled everything down to one action, one continuous movement, one thought. The crew's old mantra was running through his mind like a river, not in his own voice but in George Pocock's crisp English accent, "M-I-B, M-I-B, M-I-B."

On the train, Al Ulbrickson stared silently at the scene unfolding in front of him. A Seattle sportswriter began to holler, "Come on Washington, come on!"

Another writer shoved his paper press badge into his mouth and began to devour it. Tom Bolles was jumping up and down, beating the fellow in front of him with his lucky old fedora.

Then, in the last two hundred yards, pain suddenly came shrieking back into the boat, searing the boys' legs, their arms, their shoulders, tearing at their hearts and lungs as they desperately gulped at air. And in those last two hundred yards, in an extraordinary burst of speed, Washington passed California. With each stroke the boys took their rivals down by the length of another seat. By the time the two boats crossed the line, a glimmer of open water showed between the bow of Cal's boat and the stern of the *Husky Clipper*.

Watching from the train, Ulbrickson resumed chewing his gum. George Pocock threw back his head and howled. The sportswriter removed the chewed up remains of his press badge from his mouth. Tom Bolles continued beating the man in front of him with his lucky fedora. And in the boat the boys pumped their fists in the dark night air.

When reporters approached Ulbrickson, he stood up and said, simply. "Well, they made it close, but they won." Then he added, "I guess that little runt knew what he was doing."

Later, when they got back to the shell house, the boys found hundreds of excited fans waiting for them. They climbed out of the *Husky Clipper* and, following another rowing tradition, threw coxswain Bobby Moch into the Hudson to the delight of the spectators. After retrieving him from the water they forced their way through the crowd into the building. Ulbrickson climbed onto a bench. The boys, clutching jerseys they'd collected from the losing crews, sat on the floor around him. After a few remarks to all the rowers, proclaiming that every son and daughter of Washington was proud of them, he addressed the varsity. "Never in history has a crew given a more gallant, game fight to win the most coveted rowing honor at stake in this country than the varsity did today. And I can only say to you that I am proud and happy." He paused and looked around the room and then concluded, "I never expect to see a better rowed race." Then he stepped down. Nobody cheered. Nobody stood up and applauded. Everyone just sat, silently soaking in the moment. On the stormy night in January 1935, when Ulbrickson had first started talking openly about going to the Olympics, everyone had stood and cheered. But then it had seemed like a dream. Now they were on the verge of actually making it happen. Cheering somehow seemed dangerous.

# 22

# Here's Where We Take California

On July 1, after a week of working out and relaxing in Poughkeepsie, the boys packed up their possessions, loaded the *Husky Clipper* onto a baggage car, and headed for the 1936 U.S. Olympic trials. By six that evening, they had arrived at Princeton and entered the world of the Ivy League, the nation's oldest and most prestigious colleges. This was a world of status and tradition and wealth. It was unlike anything the boys had ever known. The young men who attended these schools weren't loggers and fishermen and farmers. They were the sons of bankers and lawyers and senators.

The boys from Washington moved into the stately Princeton Inn. From their rooms, they watched Princeton graduates stroll around the neighboring golf course wearing knickerbockers, high argyle socks, and tweed caps. The boys stopped by the Princeton Boathouse, a large and elegant stone structure, and explored Lake Carnegie. Originally, Princeton crews had rowed in a nearby canal, but the boat traffic proved troublesome, so Princeton asked the wealthy steel tycoon Andrew Carnegie to build them a lake, just for their crew. The result, Lake Carnegie, was shallow, straight, and protected. It was first-class rowing water.

Six crews were competing for the right to go to Berlin: Washington, California, the Pennsylvania Athletic Club, Navy, Princeton, and the New York Athletic Club. The field would be divided into two groups of three for the elimination heats on July 4. The top two boats in each heat would advance to a final contest of four boats the next day. The boys from Washington were not so worried about the preliminaries. They would race against Princeton and the Winged Footers of the New York Athletic Club. Neither was a real contender.

They were concerned about the finals, though. The two-thousand-meter race was less than a third the length of the four-mile Poughkeepsie competition. They weren't certain they could beat Cal at such a short distance. The start would be critical, and they'd been having trouble with their starts lately.

On Saturday, the Fourth of July, the boys left for their preliminary race a little before six thirty. It was a buggy, sultry evening. Several thousand people had gathered along the shores of the lake for the qualifying heats. A floating platform with starting stalls had been specially built for the trials. The boys backed the *Husky Clipper* into their stall and waited.

At the gun, Washington began to charge out in front almost immediately. Soon Moch told Don Hume to drop the rate. In the third minute of the race, Hume dropped it further. Even as he dropped the rate the boat began to widen its lead. By the halfway mark, Washington had open water on both boats. As they began to approach the finish line, the Winged Footers made a move, sprinting past Princeton and challenging Washington. Moch told Hume to ease the stroke rate back up. The boys from Washington pulled briskly ahead and sliced across the finish line with a two-and-a-half-length lead.

The boys were surprised at how easily they had won. Even in the muggy evening air, they'd hardly broken a sweat. Now it was time to watch the competition. They paddled out of the racing lines and took up a position along the bank at about the fifteen-hundred-meter mark. The boys wanted to see for themselves how the California crew would fare. The race was tight, but in the final five hundred meters, California executed a tremendous surge, suddenly blowing past both Navy and Penn. They won by a quarter of a boat length. And they had completed the course a full ten seconds faster than Washington had. Cal obviously was exceptional when it came to rowing two-thousand-meter sprint races.

That night, the boys were filled with anxiety. Ulbrickson went from room to room, sitting on the ends of bunks, reassuring his boys. He tried to remind them that they had in effect won a sprint in the last two thousand meters at Poughkeepsie. He was telling them what they already knew in their hearts but needed to hear one more time. They could beat any crew in America, including California, at any distance. All they had to do, he told them, was to continue to believe in one another.

Thunderstorms rumbled over New Jersey the next morning. Rain pounded the roof of the Princeton Inn. By noon, though, the day had grown hot and muggy but clear. Lake Carnegie lay mirror smooth, reflecting a translucent blue sky. The final race to determine which crew would represent the United States in Berlin was not scheduled to begin until 5:00 p.m., so the boys spent most of the day inside, trying to stay cool. Late in the afternoon, the crowds began arriving, about ten thousand people braving the heat to witness just six minutes of racing. Back in the state of Washington, people in smoky little mill towns, on soggy dairy farms, in fancy Seattle mansions, and in the Huskies' drafty shell house on Lake Washington gathered around their radios, anxious to see if their boys would be going to Berlin.

At 4:45 the crews from California, Pennsylvania, Washington, and the New York Athletic Club paddled out onto Lake Carnegie. As Washington tried to back into its stall, a large white swan blocked the way. Bobby Moch, yelling and waving his arms furiously, finally persuaded it to move slowly aside. Washington settled into position. Then California backed in.

The Washington boys were bare chested, having stripped off their jerseys just before climbing into their boat. They sat now with their oars in the water ready for the first hard pull. Each boy stared ahead at the neck of the oarsman in front of him, trying to breathe slow and easy, settling their hearts and minds into the boat. Tom Bolles had given Bobby Moch his lucky fedora. Now the coxswain reached under his seat and touched the old hat.

A little after five, the starting gun flashed.

Washington got off to a poor start. The other three boats surged ahead. The New York Athletic Club went briefly to the head of the pack, but the Pennsylvania Athletic Club quickly snatched the lead back. California settled into third place, ten feet in front of Washington's bow. After rowing hard to regain momentum but still dead last, Bobby Moch and Don Hume slowly dropped the boat's stroke rate. Yet the *Husky Clipper* held its position just behind California's stern. A quarter of the way down the course, Bobby Moch found himself creeping up on California. He told Hume to drop the rate again.

As they approached the halfway mark, the New York Athletic Club suddenly began to fade and quickly fell behind Washington. The Pennsylvania Athletic Club was in the lead. The *Husky Clipper* remained stuck on California's tail. The boys continued to row at the same rate. Don Hume and Joe Rantz were setting the pace with long, slow, sweet, fluid strokes, and the boys on each side were falling in behind them flawlessly. The boat became a single thing, gracefully and powerfully coiling and uncoiling itself, propelling itself forward. Each time the blades entered the lake, they disappeared almost without a splash or ripple.

Just before the fifteen-hundred-meter mark, Bobby Moch leaned into Don Hume and shouted, "Here's California! Here's where we take California!" Hume knocked the stroke rate up just a bit and Washington swiftly walked past Cal, seat by seat. They began to creep up on the Pennsylvania Athletic Club., then pulled even with them.

But Bobby Moch still hadn't really turned the boys loose. At last, coming inside five hundred meters, he barked at Hume. For five or six strokes, the bows of the two boats moved back and forth like the heads of racehorses coming down the stretch. Finally Washington's bow swung decisively out in front by a few feet. From there on, Washington simply blew past the exhausted rowers from the Pennsylvania Athletic Club, swinging into the last few hundred meters with extraordinary grace and power. At the finish line, they were a full length ahead and still widening the lead. As they crossed the line, Bobby Moch stood bolt upright in the stern of the shell, triumphantly thrusting one fist into the air.

All over the state of Washington, people stood and cheered. What had been a dream was now a reality. The boys from Washington were going to the Olympics. For the first time ever, Seattle was going to compete in an athletic event on the world stage. Sitting by the radio at Harry's new home on Lake Washington, Joyce and the kids cheered too. Harry said nothing, but pulled out a large American flag, tacked it on the wall above the radio, and stood back to admire it. The kids ran off to tell their friends. Joyce herself was quietly jubilant. The victory meant she would not see Joe again for months, but it would be worth the wait.

Flashing broad, white grins, Joe and his crewmates paddled back to the Princeton shell house, tossed Bobby Moch in the water, fished him out, and then lined up for the photographers. Ulbrickson said a few words, but they did not really capture the moment. Finally, he had in his grasp what had eluded him for years. Everything had come together. He had the right oarsmen, with the right attitudes, the right personalities, the right skills. Thanks to George Pocock he had a perfect boat, sleek, balanced, and wickedly fast. He had a winning strategy and a coxswain with the guts and smarts to make hard decisions and make them fast. It all added up to something far beyond the sum of its parts.

But there was a problem. That night, the chairman of the U.S. Olympic Rowing Committee, Henry Penn Burke, informed Al Ulbrickson, George Pocock, and Ray Eckman, the athletic director at Washington, that if the boys wanted to go to Berlin, they would have to pay their own way. Ulbrickson was stunned and livid. No one had hinted that the winning crew would have to fund its own trip. The university had barely been able to pay to send the boys east to Poughkeepsie and Princeton. And the boys themselves, working-class Americans, certainly didn't have the dough. Burke, who was also the chairman of the Pennsylvania Athletic

Club, noted that the Pennsylvania Athletic Club had the necessary funds. If Washington couldn't come up with five thousand dollars by the end of the week, Burke said, the crew from Pennsylvania would take its place in Berlin. As far as Ulbrickson was concerned the whole thing stank.

Late that night Ulbrickson, Pocock, Eckman, and the Washington sportswriters began making phone calls back to Seattle. The next morning, Seattleites awoke to alarming headlines and radio news bulletins, warning that their boys might not be able to afford the trip to Berlin. The entire town went to work. Students flooded the streets of downtown Seattle selling paper badges for fifty cents apiece. Money and pledges began to pour in from newspapers, companies, anonymous donors, Washington alumni, and the boys' hometowns, everywhere from Joe's Sequim to Bobby Moch's Montesano. In two days, they raised five thousand dollars. The boys from Washington were officially the United States eight-oared Olympic rowing team, and good to go to Berlin.

Joe's Olympic passport

# 23

# Rowing for Liberty

In Berlin, the preparations for the Olympics had begun several years before, back when Joe and Roger were first trying out for the freshman boat. At first, the leader of Nazi Germany, Adolf Hitler, did not want to host the games at all. Almost everything about the idea, in fact, had offended him. The very heart of the Olympic ideal was that athletes of all nations and all races should come together and compete on equal terms. But Hitler and his Nazi party believed that the Aryan people were superior to all others. The notion of Jews, blacks, and members of other races from around the world visiting his country was revolting to Hitler. Once he rose to power in 1933, however, his feelings about the Olympics began to change.

Hitler had grand plans for Germany. The country was devastated after its defeat in the First World War. The German economy had collapsed. The country's army had been outlawed. Now Hitler wanted his nation to rebuild its mili-

Berlin decked out for the Olympics

tary might, reclaim the territory it had lost in the past, and expand further across Europe and the world. He wanted the people he considered his race, the Aryan race, to reign supreme over all people. Yet he needed time to build up strength. If other nations discovered his plans before he had a chance to rebuild, they could crush those plans, so he had to keep his goals secret. One of his chief advisers, Joseph Goebbels, convinced Hitler that hosting the Olympics would be an ideal distraction. It would give the Nazis a chance to portray Germany as a civilized and modern state. The Olympics could be used to convince the world that Hitler governed a powerful but friendly nation. A country that the larger world should recognize and respect. As they put on a show of peace and progress, the Nazis could quietly restore Germany's military might and prepare to conquer Europe.

Once Hitler committed to the effort, the Olympics became a major public works project. Thousands of young German men transformed a 325-acre section outside Berlin into the Reichssportfeld, the site of the games. They constructed a great Olympic Stadium large enough to hold 110,000 people. They built a swimming stadium, an equestrian stadium, a gymnasium, tennis courts, restaurants, and more. The buildings were built with natural, German stone, and the workers were all Germans too. To get jobs Hitler decreed they had to be registered citizens and members of the Aryan race.

The Olympic rowing course lay fifteen miles to the southeast, in the leafy and pleasant lakeside community of Grünau. The rowing, canoeing, and kayaking events were all set to take place on the Langer See, one of several lakes fed by the Dahme River. The Langer See, with its deep blue water, had long been the center of water sports in Berlin. In 1925 there were dozens of rowing clubs based in and around Grünau. Some were exclusively Jewish, some only Aryan, and some happily mixed. As the Olympics approached, however, all this changed.

On September 15, 1935, Hitler stood before the leaders of the German government and announced three new laws. First, the Nazi party emblem, the swastika, was to become the official flag of Germany. Second, only people of German or related blood could be citizens of Germany. The third law was aimed directly at Jews. Among other things, it prohibited the marriage of Jews and non-Jews. In the next few months and years, Germany's government would add dozens of additional laws restricting every aspect of the lives of German Jews, taking away even their most basic freedoms. Across Germany, in towns and cities, signs proclaiming "Juden unerwünscht" ("Jews not welcome") appeared over the entrances to hotels, drugstores, public swimming pools, and shops of all sorts. Books written by Jewish authors and others the Nazis did not like were burned in public places. In Grünau, Jewish rowing clubs were banned. Others clubs were threatened if they did not kick out their Jewish rowers. Men who had rowed with one another for a lifetime began to turn their backs on their former crewmates and neighbors. Forbidding signs went up over the doors of shell houses. Doors were locked, keys changed.

These frightening developments had not gone unnoticed outside Germany. In the United States, there was a movement to boycott the 1936 Olympics in protest over the treatment of Jews in Germany. On November 21, 1935, ten thousand anti-Nazi demonstrators marched peacefully through New York City, calling for America to stay home from the games. In December, the Amateur Athletic Union of the United States voted on a new resolution. If the vote passed, the group would send a three-man committee to Germany to investigate claims that Nazis were mistreating Jews. But the vote failed. There would be no investigation. The boycott effort was effectively dead, and American athletes prepared to go to Berlin for the 1936 Olympics.

After Princeton, the New York Athletic Club invited Ulbrickson and the crew to use its training facilities at Travers Island, an elegant spot on the nearby Long Island Sound. The club had a formal dining room and an oyster bar, a full-featured gymnasium, a boathouse, a baseball diamond, a bowling alley, a barbershop, and every conceivable sort of athletic training equipment. The boys had easy access to excellent rowing water on the sound. And, best of all, for boys from the fields, forests, and small towns of the Pacific Northwest, it was just a few miles from the glamour and excitement of New York City.

The nation was in the grip of the greatest heat wave in its history, but the boys didn't let the sweltering heat stop them from visiting major sites like Rocke-feller Center and Wall Street, the source of the great stock market crash of 1929 that had begun the Great Depression. They rode the subway out to the beach at Coney Island. They made their way through the crowds on the boardwalk. They shoveled down five-cent hot dogs at Nathan's, ate cotton candy, guzzled ice-cold Coca Cola, gobbled peanuts, rode the hair-raising Cyclone roller coaster. And in Times Square one afternoon, a tall, somewhat heavy man rushed up to Shorty, took a good look, and said, "You're Shorty Hunt!" He looked at the other boys. "You fellows are the Washington crew, aren't you?" He gushed that he had rec-ognized Shorty from a picture in the newspaper. For the first time the boys sud-denly felt like celebrities. And something else began to dawn on them. They were beginning to understand that they were not just the University of Washington crew anymore. They were America's crew. The *W* on their jerseys was about to be replaced with *USA*.

They were rowing for something larger now. This fact struck Bobby Moch as he was sitting in the shade under a tree in a wide-open field on Travers Island, opening an envelope from his father. The envelope contained a letter listing the addresses of the relatives he hoped to visit in Europe, as he had requested. But it also contained a second, sealed envelope labeled, "Read this in a private place." Now, alarmed, Moch opened the second envelope and read its contents. Gaston Moch told his son that when he met his relatives in Europe, he was going to learn for the first time that he was Jewish. Bobby sat under the tree, brooding for a long while. He was not upset that he was Jewish. He was bothered by the fact that his father had felt it necessary to conceal his heritage from his friends, his neighbors, and even his own children. Now Bobby was heading off to race in a country that was gradually making it illegal even to be Jewish at all.

For Joe, the moment of clarity came on the eighty-sixth floor of the new Empire State Building. None of the boys had ever ridden an elevator more than a few floors in a hotel, and the rapid ascent to the eighty-sixth floor of the Empire State Building thrilled them nearly as much as the roller coaster out at Coney Island. Standing on the observation deck, Joe looked out at the many spires of New York rising through the smoke and steam and haze. He had never seen anything like it, and he did not know whether he found it beautiful or frightening.

He dropped a nickel in a telescope for a better view of the Brooklyn Bridge, then swept the telescope across Lower Manhattan and out to the distant Statue of Liberty. In a few days, he would be sailing under her on his way to Germany, a place where liberty was not a given right. The headlines about the Nazis were impossible to ignore. Joe didn't know all the details, but as he understood it, liberty was under some kind of assault in Germany.

For the first time, Joe realized that he and the boys would not just be rowing for gold. They would be rowing for a way of life, a shared set of values. Liberty was perhaps the most important of those values. But to the boys from Washington, America also stood for trust in one another, for mutual respect, for humility, and for fair play. These ideals were part of what had drawn them together as a crew. And they were about to show the world the power of those ideals when they took to the water at Grünau.

George Pocock spent the last few days before their departure for Germany carefully sanding down the hull of the *Husky Clipper*, then applying coat after coat of marine varnish, buffing each coat until the shell glistened. He wasn't doing it just for looks. The race in Berlin could come down to fractions of a second. He wanted the shell to have the fastest racing surface possible.

On July 13, Pocock supervised the boys as they carefully loaded the sixty-two-foot *Husky Clipper* onto a long truck and drove it through the heart of New York City with a police escort. They pulled up alongside the SS *Manhattan*, the 668-foot-long ship that would transport 334 members of the U.S. Olympic team to Germany, and searched for a place to stow their shell. It took them an hour to figure out a way to hoist it up to the boat deck. Then they tied it down, covered it with a tarp, and hoped and prayed that no one would mistake it for a bench.

The SS Manhattan

On the boat to Berlin

Two days later, with cameras rolling and flashbulbs popping, the boys bounded up the gangplank and onto the *Manhattan* at ten thirty in the morning. They were giddy, charged with excitement. After stowing their gear and meeting some of the other athletes, they joined hundreds of others waving American flags up on deck. As the noon departure time approached, more than ten thousand spectators crowded onto the pier at the edge of the Hudson River. Blimps and airplanes circled overhead. Black smoke began to billow out of the red, white, and blue smokestacks of the *Manhattan*.

The crowd on the dock, waving their hats over their heads, began a thunderous chant: "'Ray! 'Ray! 'Ray! For the USA!" A band struck up a tune, the lines were cast off, and the *Manhattan* began to back slowly out into the Hudson. Joe and the other boys rushed to the rails, waving their flags, taking up the chant. The whistles on tugs and ferries and nearby ships began to shriek. Out on the river, fireboats let loose with their sirens and shot white plumes of water high into the air.

As the boat passed the Statue of Liberty and cruised out into the Atlantic, Joe stayed on deck, leaning on the rail, enjoying the cool air. He was trying to remember everything so he could tell Joyce all about it when he returned home. Hours later, when the sun had begun to set in the west, Joe retreated into the ship, looking for the rest of the boys and food. The *Manhattan*—her lights ablaze and loud with music and the laughter of young people at play—sailed forward, out into the darkness of the North Atlantic, on its way to Hitler's Germany.

Joe's Olympic jersey

# 24

# Fighting, Fuming, and Coming Together

As Joe drifted into sleep aboard the *Manhattan* that night, the first light of dawn crept over Berlin, where Nazi police and soldiers were marching groups of men, woman, and children through the streets at gunpoint. The arrests had begun hours earlier, under the veil of night. The Nazis were moving Gypsy families living in shanties and wagons out of a Berlin suburb and into detention camps. In time they would be sent east to death camps and murdered.

Their removal was just one more step in a process that had been unfolding for months. The Nazis were transforming Berlin into something like a vast movie set, an artificial world with all the horror and anti-Semitism hidden away. The signs prohibiting Jews from entering public facilities had been taken down and stored for later use. A fiercely anti-Jewish newspaper had been temporarily removed from newsstands. Fourteen hundred homeless people had been rounded up and removed from the streets. Shop windows had been polished. Streets had been swept and reswept, trains freshly painted, broken windows replaced. Books banned by the Nazis temporarily reappeared in bookshop windows. Joseph Goebbels, the man who helped convince Hitler to host the games, handed locals a script for their performance when they met foreigners, instructing them to be charming, easygoing, and welcoming to all.

On the *Manhattan*, the trip over was difficult for Don Hume and Roger Morris. Hume had developed some kind of cold in Princeton. Now he and Morris became terribly seasick. But Joe was enjoying himself. He was meeting other Olympians and eating all the food he could find.

The athletes were expected to remain in the tourist-class areas of the boat. First class was supposed to be for the sort of people Joe had seen on the golf courses at Princeton. But the boys didn't think much of this class business. Soon they were prowling on plush carpeting through a maze of corridors leading to spacious cabins with wood paneling, a smoking lounge with a wood-burning fireplace, and a grand ballroom with high white plastered ceilings, marble columns, and delicately hand-painted murals. They found the first-class dining room with its own orchestra balcony and dining tables draped with elegant tablecloths. And they found the Grand Salon, where movies were shown every evening. Soon they discovered that when five or six large young men who just happened to be Olympic oarsmen sat in the Grand Salon, nobody was about to remove them. So they took to visiting the upper decks every evening, stopping on their way into the Grand Salon to swipe a platter of hors d'oeuvres and then passing it around as they watched the show.

One afternoon Joe returned to his cabin to find his new rowing uniform. There was a pair of white shorts and an elegant white jersey with a U.S. Olympic shield. Red, white, and blue ribbons were stitched around the neck and down the front. The fabric of the jersey was smooth, almost like silk. He held it up for a better look and it shimmered in the light streaming in through his porthole. The jersey immediately meant the world to Joe. He had never been beaten. He had never been obliged to follow the old custom of surrendering his jersey to a rival oarsman. He had no intention of letting this jersey be the first. Joe Rantz was taking this one home.

On the morning of July 24 the ship docked in Hamburg, Germany. The boys awoke early to unload the *Husky Clipper*. They were edgy, anxious to get off the boat. Except for Don Hume, who was still fighting some kind of cold, they had put on five or six pounds each during the nine-day voyage. They were starting to feel flabby and out of shape. They wanted to stretch their arms and climb into a racing shell. By noon they were on a train to Berlin, and when they arrived in the city's palatial old Lehrter Station that afternoon, they were stunned. Thousands of Germans had packed the station to get a glimpse of them. A black locomotive with swastikas emblazoned on its sides loomed nearby. A brass band struck up a song. The athletes boarded open-top buses and followed a parade route through the city. Tens of thousands of Germans cheered and waved Olympic, Nazi, and occasionally even American flags.

Later that afternoon, the boys finally arrived at what would be their home for the next several weeks, a police cadet training academy in Köpenick, a quaint village a few miles away from the Olympic rowing course. Unlike most of the ancient buildings in town, the police academy was modern looking—all glass,

The U.S. Olympic team arrives in Berlin

steel, and concrete. Most of the cadets had been moved out to make room for the American oarsmen and others. Unfortunately, even though the building was brand-new, it was cold and there were no hot showers.

The next morning, the boys awoke early, eager to get out on the water. After breakfast a gray German army bus transported them three miles down the Langer See to the racecourse in Grünau. When they arrived, the boys discovered that they were going to share a shell house with the German crew—a fine new brick and stucco building called Haus West. Over the entrance, an American flag and a Nazi flag faced each other. The German oarsmen were courteous but hardly gushing with enthusiasm to meet the boys from Washington. They seemed to be a bit older, and they were exceptionally fit and disciplined. They were almost military in the way they carried themselves.

When the boys finally took to the water, the results were spectacularly disappointing. Their timing was all off. Their pulls were weak and inefficient. The Canadian and Australian crews, practicing sprints, blew past them with smirks on their faces. Ulbrickson had never seen them row so poorly. The boys had gained a lot of weight and almost all of them had colds. Don Hume's seemed to be getting worse, and the chilling winds on the Langer See and cold, drafty police barracks hardly helped.

Over the next few days, the boys fell into a routine: rowing badly in the morning and then heading into Berlin for the afternoon. They took in shows, visited tourist sites, and bought bratwurst sausages from street vendors. Over and over again, ordinary Germans greeted them by extending their right hands palms down and shouting, "Heil Hitler!" The boys took to responding by extending their own hands and saluting their own leader, President Roosevelt. They'd shout, "Heil Roosevelt!" The Germans, for the most part, pretended not to notice.

But those afternoon jaunts weren't enough to improve the crew's morale. They were still rowing terribly. Gordy Adam and Don Hume were still sick. By July 29, Hume was too ill to row. Too ill, in fact, to get out of bed. Ulbrickson put Don Coy, a substitute who had made the trip, in at the critical stroke position. But when they practiced with Coy in the stroke seat, the boat just didn't feel right.

Ulbrickson was deeply concerned now. As crews from other nations arrived at Grünau, he and Pocock were spending a lot of time down by the water, studying the competition. The Germans had to be taken very seriously. The Italians also looked like a threat. They had lost to California in the 1932 Olympics by only two-tenths of a second. Now four of the rowers from that boat were back for another chance. The Japanese crew, from Tokyo Imperial University, rowed in a small shell, with short oars and small blades, and they averaged just 145 pounds per oarsman. But they could accelerate at an astonishing rate. The Australians did not boast the best technique, but they had fire and strength.

Above all, though, Pocock and Ulbrickson believed the British were the boat to beat. Rowing was traditionally a British sport, and the oarsmen and coxswain that Britain had sent to the 1936 Olympics were the best of the British best. William George Ranald Mundell Laurie, also known as Ran, was perhaps the best British stroke of his generation. He was 188 pounds of power, grace, and keen intelligence. Along with coxswain John Noel Duckworth, a small man with great heart, Laurie had piloted his crew to three major victories in a row. In the famed Boat Race on the Thames River in London, they'd already raced and won in front of a half million to a million fans. To Ulbrickson, that experience alone had to give the British boys an edge.

What most concerned Ulbrickson about the British boys, though, was their strategy. They liked to do exactly what the Washington boys did so well. They excelled at sitting back but staying close, rowing hard but slow, then mowing down their opponents in the end. Duckworth operated an awful lot like Bobby Moch. And Ran Laurie handled the stroke oar an awful lot like Don Hume. It was going to be interesting to see what happened when two crews playing the same game met on the Langer See.

The 1936 games opened officially on August 1, in a spectacular ceremony at the Olympic Stadium, but the rowing competition would not begin until August 12.

As the boys waited, the weather on the Langer See turned positively wintry. A cold, cutting wind blew down the racecourse. The boys rowed in sweat shirts, their legs slathered in goose grease to protect them from the chill. The preliminary heats were less than two weeks away, but they still hadn't regained their form. Their timing was off. They caught crabs. They were out of shape, and Don Hume wasn't getting any healthier. Since he'd first gotten sick at Princeton, he had never really stopped coughing and dragging around. Unless he got healthy, Ulbrickson figured they would not have a chance. And then there was the matter of the racecourse. Ulbrickson was not happy with how it had been laid out. There were six lanes. If there was a strong wind on race day, the two outermost lanes would be so exposed that the crews stuck there would have a much harder row. Lanes one through three, on the other hand, stuck close to the southern shore of the lake. They were protected from the wind through most of the course. The crews assigned to these lanes would basically have a two-length advantage over the boats on the outside. Ulbrickson wanted the outer lanes eliminated, but German Olympic officials rejected the idea.

As the heats approached, Ulbrickson grounded the boys. There would be no more trips into Berlin or anywhere else. The boys began to get tense and fidgety again. Nerves began to grow raw among the other crews as well. The Aussies made no effort to conceal their contempt for the Brits. The Brits could not even look at the Germans. They remembered fighting them in the last war, and they were worried a second one was coming soon.

At lunchtime one day, the tensions erupted. The different crews ate together, and it had become a tradition for them to sing national songs during meals. When it came time for the Yugoslavian crew to rise and sing, they launched into an odd rendition of "Yankee Doodle." There was something about the way they sang that Chuck Day did not appreciate. He was convinced they were insulting the United States of America. And he would not stand for that.

Day bolted out of his seat and plowed into the Yugoslavians, fists flying. Bobby Moch charged right in behind him, going for the biggest man on the crew. Right behind Moch came the rest of the Washington boys, and behind them, just for the fun of it, the entire Australian team. The German crew rushed to the side of the Yugoslavians. Boys shoved other boys. They threw chairs and hurled insults. A few more fists flew. Everyone was yelling, but because of all the different languages, nobody could understand what anybody else was saying. Finally the Dutch national crew dove in and settled everyone down.

In the last few days before the first preliminary heat the American boys worked on centering and calming themselves. None of them wanted to waste his chance at a gold medal. And none wanted to waste it for the others. All along Joe Rantz had figured he was the weak link in the crew. He'd been added to the boat last. He had often struggled to master the technical side of the sport. But what Joe didn't know was that every boy in the boat felt exactly the same way. Every one of them believed he was simply lucky to be rowing in the boat, that he didn't really measure up to the obvious greatness of the other boys, and that he might fail the others at any moment. None of them wanted to let that happen.

The boys began to draw even closer together. They took to huddling on the float before and after workouts, talking about what, precisely, they could do to improve. They draped arms over one another's shoulders and talked through their race plan, speaking softly but with increasing confidence. They looked one another in the eye, speaking earnestly. They quoted Pocock to one another.

Left to right: Joe Rantz, Stub McMillin, Bobby Moch, Chuck Day, Shorty Hunt

They walked the shores of the lake, skipping stones, but the jokes and horseplay were gone now. They began to grow serious in a way they had never been before. Hume returned to the boat, and everything began to feel right again. They began to find their swing.

They were back. All they needed now, Pocock told them on August 10, was a little competition. And they were about to get it.

View from the grandstands at Grünau

# 25

# A Game of Cat and Mouse

There were fourteen eight-oared crews, and each would have
two chances to make it into the race for the gold on August 14. If a given crew
won its preliminary race on August 12, it would earn a spot in the medal round
automatically. Each of the losing crews would race again on August 13 and
would need to win that heat to advance to the final on the following day. For
their preliminary race, the boys from Washington were assigned to row against
France, Japan, Czechoslovakia, and the crew they were most concerned about,
Great Britain.

Now that the boat was performing well, Ulbrickson backed off the training
and told the boys to rest. This did little to help Don Hume, though. By race day,
he was ill again. He had lost a total of fourteen pounds. His six-foot-two frame
was down to skin and bones. His chest was still congested, and he was running
a fever on and off. But he insisted he was ready to row. On the day of the prelim-

inary, he stayed in bed until late afternoon, when the boys boarded the bus for the racecourse.

Conditions were almost ideal for rowing. The skies were lightly overcast, but the temperatures were in the low seventies. Only a hint of wind out on the Langer See ruffled the slate-gray water. The boys had been assigned to row in lane one, the most protected from what little wind there was. By the time Joe and the boys paddled to the starting line, some twenty-five thousand people had entered the regatta grounds. The boys backed the *Husky Clipper* into position and waited. Right next door, in lane two, Ran Laurie, Noel Duckworth, and the rest of the British crew did the same. Duckworth nodded at Bobby Moch, and Moch returned the gesture.

The race started, and the American boys got away badly again. Someone in the middle of the boat missed the water on the first or second stroke. In lane four the Japanese fluttered rapidly into the lead, whipping at the water. Noel Duckworth and Ran Laurie took the British boat out hard but then eased up and settled into second place behind the Japanese. The United States was dead last. Once they got going, Moch and Hume kept the stroke rate high until they passed the Czechs. Then they eased up too. The Japanese stretched their lead over the British to a full length. But neither Moch nor Duckworth was thinking about the Japanese. They were thinking about each other. And until the halfway point they held their positions.

The exhausted Japanese suddenly began to fade, along with the Czechs. So did the French. That left the Americans and the Brits right where they had expected to be, alone with each other at the front of the pack. Now it was a game of cat and mouse.

Moch told Hume to edge the rate up slightly, to see what would happen. Hume kicked it up to thirty-six. The U.S. boat crept to within a half length of the British boat's stern. Duckworth glanced over his shoulder. He and Laurie picked up the pace. The British boat held its lead. The boys in both boats could now hear the roar of the crowd in the grandstands. The coxswains could see the finish line up ahead. But neither was ready to make his move yet. Both were holding back.

Finally, with 250 meters to go, Moch shouted, "Now, boys. Now! Give me ten!" The boys dug hard. The American flag snapping at the front of the *Husky Clipper* began to move past Duckworth, creeping halfway up the length of the British boat. For a moment, they held their position, the white blades of the U.S. shell flashing furiously alongside the crimson blades of the British. Then Moch yelped at Hume to up the rate again, and the *Clipper* resumed advancing.

The British remained out front by half a length with 150 meters to go. But the American boys had found their swing and they were holding on to it. They were rowing as hard as they had ever rowed, taking huge sweeping cuts at the water, over and over again, rocking into the beat as if they were forged together. Every muscle, tendon, and ligament in their bodies was burning with pain. But they were rowing in perfect, flawless harmony. Nothing was going to stop them. In the last twenty strokes, they simply powered past the British boat. The American fans in the stands rose and cheered as the bow of the *Husky Clipper* knifed across the line a full twenty feet ahead of the British shell. A moment later, Don Hume pitched forward and collapsed across his oar.

It took Moch a full minute of splashing water on Hume's face before Hume was able to sit upright again and help paddle the shell over to the float. When they got there, though, the boys got sweet news. Their time, 6:00.8, was a new Olympic and world record. Ulbrickson crouched down next to the boat and quietly said, "Well done, boys."

As the boys tucked into their dinners that night at the police academy in Köpenick, they were jubilant. The British would have to row and win the next day to make the finals, but the Americans would have a day off. Al Ulbrickson, though, remained deeply concerned. After dinner he ordered Don Hume back to his sickbed. The boy looked like death. Whatever he had, it was clearly more than a cold. Now Ulbrickson had to figure out who was going to stroke the boat when they raced again in two days.

After lunch the next day, the boys wandered through town, joking, poking into shops, taking pictures, buying a few souvenirs, exploring corners of Köpenick they hadn't yet seen. Like most of the Americans in Berlin that summer, they had concluded that the new Germany was a pretty nice place. It was clean, the people were friendly, everything worked neatly and efficiently, and the girls were pretty.

But there was a Germany the boys could not see, a Germany that was hidden from them. Three years earlier, the waters of the Langer See had been reddened with blood. In 1933, Nazi soldiers rounded up hundreds of Köpenick's Jews, Catholics, and others, tortured ninety-one of them to death, then dumped their bodies into the river Spree and the Langer See. And even as the boys explored the town, to the north of Berlin the Germans were already constructing a sprawling concentration camp. Tens of thousands of prisoners would soon die there.

As the boys walked the streets that afternoon, they did not know that many of the locals they passed were doomed. People who waited on them in shops. Old women strolling around the grounds of Köpenick's castle. Mothers pushing baby carriages on cobblestone streets. Children shrieking gleefully on playgrounds. Old men walking dogs. Before long, many of them would be shipped off on trains, sent to their deaths. During the Olympics, though, the brutal reality of Nazi Germany was nearly invisible. To the athletes, Köpenick seemed to be about as pleasant and peaceful as anything back home in Washington.

That evening the boys went down to the course to watch the next set of races, the heats that would determine the final lineup for the medal race. Hungary and Switzerland were already through, and now Germany, Italy, and Great Britain each won their races. The boys finally knew who they were going to have to beat to win gold. The one remaining question was which lane they'd be assigned to, and when Al Ulbrickson found out, he was furious. Normally, the team with the top time earned the most favorable lane. So Ulbrickson figured his boys would be rowing in lane one, which was protected from the wind. Instead, the German Olympic Committee changed the rules for the finals. The Germans were given the best lane. Italy was in lane two and Switzerland in lane three. Hungary had lane four. Great Britain was in lane five. And the United States was all the way out in lane six.

The protected lanes went to the host country and her closest ally. The worst lanes went to her potential enemies, Great Britain and the United States. It was deeply suspicious, and just what Ulbrickson had feared since first seeing the course. If there was any kind of headwind the next day, his boys were going to have to make up as much as two boat lengths just to get even with the field.

The weather did not seem willing to cooperate. The next morning a cold, steady rain was falling in Grünau, and a blustery wind was whipping down the race-course. At the police academy in Köpenick, the jubilation had evaporated. Don Hume was still in bed, his fever spiking once again, and Al Ulbrickson had decided he could not row. Don Coy, the substitute, would have to step into the shell again at the stroke position. Ulbrickson broke the news to Hume, then to the others.

At the breakfast table, the boys ate scrambled eggs and steak, sitting silently, their eyes seeing nothing and no one. This was the day that they had worked for all year. In fact, most had worked for three years to get here. Now it had all come down to one final race, and they were not going to be together. They began to talk it over, and the more they talked, the more certain they were. It just wasn't right. Hume had to be there with them. They weren't just nine guys in a boat. They were a single thing, a crew. They got up and went to Ulbrickson. Stub Mc-Millin was the team captain now, so he cleared his throat and nervously stepped forward. Hume was absolutely vital to the rhythm of the boat, he told his coach. Nobody else could respond as quickly and smoothly to the moment-by-moment adjustments that a crew had to make during a race. Bobby Moch piped up. He just had to have Hume sitting in front of him, responding to his calls, setting the pace. He and Hume could almost read each other's minds. Then Joe stepped forward: "If you put him in the boat, Coach, we will pull him across the line. Just strap him in. He can just go along for the ride."

Outside, a German army bus was waiting to take them down to Grünau for the medal race. Ulbrickson told them to go get their gear. The boys began to troop upstairs. After a long few moments, Ulbrickson shouted up the stairwell after them, "And bring Hume along with you!"

Ulbrickson's final advice

# 26

# In the Race of Their Lives

By early afternoon the rain had still not let up in Grünau. The Langer See was rough, the wind brisk out on the water, the scene dark and gloomy. But in those days, rowing was one of the most popular Olympic events, and tens of thousands of spectators, most of them German, began to flood into the regatta grounds. They huddled under black umbrellas. They wore black slickers and hats. They filled the massive wooden bleachers on one side of the course, stood shoulder to shoulder at the water's edge, and took refuge under the cover of the huge permanent grandstand at the finish line. As the start of the first race approached, more than seventy-five thousand fans had packed the regatta grounds, the largest crowd ever to witness an Olympic rowing event.

The eight-oared competition was the main event, but not the only rowing race that day. At 2:30 p.m., the four-man race began. The Swiss jumped out to an early lead but were soon overtaken by the German boat. Inside the shell house, the American boys were waiting. They'd laid Don Hume out on a massage table like a corpse, bundling him in overcoats to keep him warm and dry. As the boats in the first race approached the finish, they could hear the roar of the crowd. The fans chanted Germany's name, "Deutschland! Deutschland! Deutschland!" And Germany sliced across the finish line a full eight seconds ahead of the Swiss. Then the boys heard another, deeper, more guttural roar rising from the crowd, and a different chant: "Sieg Heil! Sieg Heil! Sieg Heil!"

Adolf Hitler had entered the regatta grounds, followed by a large entourage of Nazi officials. Wearing a dark uniform and a full-length rain cape, he made his way up a staircase and took his place of honor on the wide balcony looking down on the crowd and the Langer See. He held up his right hand. The crowd continued to thunder "Sieg Heil!" until Hitler lowered his hand. Only then did the racing resume.

The crowd soon had plenty of opportunity to make more noise. In event after event that afternoon, German oarsmen charged down the course ahead of their competition, winning gold medals in the first five races. Each time, the Nazi flag was raised at the end of the race, and the crowd sang the national anthem, "Deutschland über alles," or "Germany above all," a little more loudly. Hitler's chief lieutenants, including Joseph Goebbels and Hermann Göring, his main military adviser, celebrated with each victory. Hitler himself, peering through his binoculars, simply nodded enthusiastically each time a German boat crossed the line in first place. He believed his people were superior. These triumphs were expected.

The rain began to taper off. The skies lightened. And the crowd was in a frenzy. It looked as if Germany would sweep the day. Then, in the sixth race,

German fans waiting in the rain

the British pair of Jack Beresford and Dick Southwood rallied terrifically in the final 250 meters and won by almost six seconds. For the first time all day, a queer hush fell over the regatta course at Grünau. In the shell house, George Pocock was looking over the *Husky Clipper* when he paused for a moment and realized suddenly that he was listening to the British anthem, "God Save the King." Out of habit, he stood bolt upright, filled with pride.

As the final event grew near, the crowd began to grow noisy once more. The eight-oared race was the rowing event that nations boasted about. This was the ultimate test of young men's ability to pull together. It was the greatest display of power, grace, and guts on water.

A little before six, Don Hume got up from the massage table. He joined the rest of the boys as they hoisted the *Husky Clipper* to their shoulders and walked down to the water. The Germans and Italians were already in their boats. The Italians were wearing silky light blue uniforms, and they had tied white scarves around their heads, pirate-style. The Germans wore white shorts and white jerseys, each emblazoned with a black eagle and swastika on the front. The American boys were wearing mismatched track shorts and tattered old sweatshirts. They didn't want to get their new uniforms dirty.

Bobby Moch tucked Tom Bolles's lucky fedora beneath his seat in the stern of his shell. The boys huddled briefly with Ulbrickson, reviewing the race plan, then stepped into their boat and paddled up the lake toward the starting line. Ulbrickson and Pocock climbed up to a balcony of a shell house near the finish line. They were worried. Their boys were good. But with Don Hume looking like a dead man and the crew stuck out in lane six, they figured their chances of taking gold were slim to none.

In Seattle it was early morning. Harry Rantz had risen before dawn and made coffee and turned the radio on, just to make sure it was working. Joyce had come over a bit later and gotten the kids up. Now they were all in the kitchen, eating oatmeal, trying to steady their nerves. All over America millions of people were tuning their radios to listen in. If they were lucky enough to have a job, they were going in to work a little late. If they were lucky enough to still have a farm, they were putting off their chores until later.

The story of the track star Jesse Owens had already excited much of the country. Owens, an African American man, won four gold medals in Berlin, dominating the track-and-field competition and defying Hitler's theory of the Aryan race's supremacy. Owens's victories infuriated the Nazis. Back home, his accomplishments—and Hitler's angry reaction—reminded America what the Nazis stood for. Americans realized that there was more at stake in these Olympic Games than a few medals. A way of life was at stake. Basic fairness was at stake. Some Americans had never even heard of Seattle before the Poughkeepsie Regatta, but now millions waited anxiously to see what the rough-and-tumble western boys from Washington would do as Hitler looked on.

At 9:15 a.m. in Seattle, as the radio commentary began, Joyce rummaged through her purse and pulled out a small book. She flipped through its pages and carefully extracted a delicate green four-leaf clover. Joe had given it to her years before, and she had pressed it between the book's pages. Now she laid it atop the radio, pulled up a chair, and started to listen.

On the Langer See, the boys rowed toward the starting line. Rain showers had begun to slant down out of the sky again. But the rain wasn't the problem. They were from Seattle. They'd rowed through much worse rain. The wind, however, was gusting on and off, pushing in bursts and fits at the starboard side of the shell. Up front, Roger Morris and Chuck Day were having a hard time keeping the boat on an even keel. Bobby Moch was manipulating the rudder, desperately trying to keep the shell on a straight course. He didn't like the wind, and he didn't like the looks of Don Hume. He was just paddling, not putting much into his strokes.

Joe Rantz felt pretty good, though. As the noise of the crowd fell away behind them, the world in the shell had grown quiet and calm. It seemed to be past time for words. Joe and the boys in the middle of the boat were just rocking gently back and forth, rowing slow and low, breathing in and out comfortably. The boat felt easy under them, sleek and lithe. For Joe, anxiety gave way to a sense of calm. He was more determined than nervous. If Don Hume had the guts to row this race, Joe and the boys were not going to let him down.

They pulled the shell into position, backing against a gangway. They were out in the middle of the Langer See. Ahead of them the lake was wide open. The wind was worse than it had been down in front of the grandstands. It pushed at their bow, slapping small, choppy waves against the port side. Roger Morris and Gordy Adam were struggling, stroking in place on the starboard side, trying to lever the boat back against the wind and keep the bow pointed more or less down the middle of the lane. In the next lane over, the British boat backed into position.

They waited for the start. Bobby Moch hollered instructions up front to Roger and Gordy, who were still focused on straightening the bow. Behind them, and out of sight, the official starter suddenly emerged, holding a flag aloft. Almost immediately, he turned slightly in the direction of lanes one and two, the Germans and the Italians. Then he shouted into the wind, in French—"*Partez!*"—and dropped the flag.

Bobby Moch never heard him. Never saw the flag. Neither, apparently, did British coxswain Noel Duckworth. Four boats surged forward. The British and the Americans, for a horrific moment, sat motionless at the line, dead in the water.

Out of the corner of his eye, Joe saw the Hungarian boat leap forward. A split second later, he saw the British boat do the same. He bellowed, "Let's get out of here!" Bobby Moch barked, "Row!" All eight American oars dug into the water. For another fraction of a second, the *Husky Clipper* sagged slightly under the boys as nearly a ton of dead weight resisted being put in motion. Then the boat sprang forward, and the boys were away. They were already a stroke and a half behind in the race of their lives.

Bobby Moch had planned to come from behind, as always. But the spectacularly bad start meant that the two-length handicap of being in lane six was even greater now. Moch needed to build up some momentum, and he needed to do it quickly. He shouted at Hume to hit it hard. Hume set a high pace and the boys dug hard and fast.

The Germans and Italians moved briskly to the front of the field. The British boat charged furiously back. At the rear of the field, the American boat began to claw its way forward. As the first boats crossed the hundred-meter mark, an announcer called out the standings, and the crowd roared when they heard the Germans were in the lead. The Americans were still in last place, but only a length and a half behind the Germans. Bobby Moch told Hume to ease off on the rate a bit. They were still nearly sprinting, but Moch figured that with the wind they had to row at a high rate just to stay in contention. He could only hope they'd still have something left for the real sprint at the end. The boys began to settle in.

As they moved out into the widest part of the Langer See, the wind grew even stronger. Waves splashed over the small American flag near the bow of the *Husky Clipper*. Moch struggled to steer the boat in the wind. Switzerland claimed the lead. At two hundred meters, the British surged past Germany and into second place. Bobby Moch watched them but he didn't take the bait. It was fine with him if the Brits wanted to burn themselves out in the first half of the race.

The German eight

Then, three hundred meters out, Moch saw something that chilled him to his core. Don Hume suddenly went white in the face and all but closed his eyes. His mouth fell open. Moch yelled at him, "Don! Are you okay?" Hume didn't respond. Moch couldn't tell if he was about to pass out or just in some kind of zone. Either way, it didn't look right. The way he looked, Moch wasn't sure if Hume could even finish the race, let alone sprint when the time for sprinting came.

The boats were approaching the five-hundred-meter mark now, a quarter of the way down the racecourse. Switzerland, Britain, and Germany were tied for the lead. The Americans and Italians were a boat length behind them. Hungary was last. The boats in the inside lanes were moving into the protected part of the lake now, where the water was nearly flat. But the American boys were still being slammed by the winds, spray flying from their oars every time they popped out of the water. The pain started to build. Very slowly they began to fall farther back. By eight hundred meters, they were dead last again.

Over in the sheltered water of lane two, Italy came up from the rear and took a narrow lead over Germany. The bow of the Italian boat sliced across the halfway point. A bell began to toll, signaling the spectators at the finish that the crews were approaching. Seventy-five thousand people rose to their feet. On the balcony of the main shell house, Haus West, Hitler, Goebbels, and Göring pressed their binoculars to their eyes. Next door, Al Ulbrickson saw the *Husky Clipper* struggling down the outside lane. The announcer called out the thousand-meter-split times. The crowd roared. Italy was in first, but Germany was close behind. Ulbrickson's boys were behind by nearly five full seconds.

In the stern of the *Husky Clipper*, Bobby Moch knew he couldn't afford to wait any longer. He hunched forward and bellowed for Hume to take the stroke

The Italian eight

rate up. "Higher!" he shouted into Hume's face. "Higher!" Nothing happened. "Higher, Don! Higher!" he screamed, pleading now. Hume's head rocked back and forth with the rhythm of the boat, as if he were about to nod off. He seemed to be staring at something on the floor of the boat. Moch couldn't even make eye contact with him.

Germany retook the lead. Another enormous roar went up from the crowd. Then the roaring turned into chanting. The crowd was cheering in time with the stroke rate of the German boat. "Deutsch-land! Deutsch-land! Deutsch-land!" On his balcony Hitler rocked back and forth with the chant.

In Seattle a hush fell over Harry Rantz's living room when Joe's family heard the times.

In the boat, Joe had no idea how things stood, except that he was vaguely aware that he hadn't seen any boats falling away behind him. He knew that meant they were trailing the field, but he also knew it wasn't because they'd been rowing easy. He had been rowing hard against the wind all the way. His arms and legs were starting to feel as if they were encased in cement. It was too early for the sprint, but he was starting to wonder what would happen when Moch called for it. How much would he have left? How much would any of them have left?

Moch was growing desperate. Hume still wasn't responding. The only option Moch had left was to hand the stroke's responsibility off to Joe. It would be a dangerous move that could throw everyone off, but if he could just get Joe to set a higher rate, maybe Hume would sense the change and pick it up. Moch had to do something, and with the finish line approaching, he had to do it now.

As Moch leaned forward to tell Joe to raise the rate, Don Hume's head snapped up, his eyes popped open, he clamped his mouth shut, and he looked at

Bobby Moch straight in the eyes. A startled Moch yelled, "Pick'er up! Pick'er up!" This time Hume responded. Moch yelled again, "One length to make up—six hundred meters to go!" The boys leaned into their oars. The stroke rate jumped, and then jumped again, climbing higher and higher. At the fifteen-hundred-me-ter mark, the *Husky Clipper* eased from fifth to third place. But they were still nearly a full length behind Germany and Italy.

The Langer See narrowed. The *Husky Clipper* finally sliced into water that was protected from the wind by tall trees and buildings. Conditions were even now. The game was on. But there were only 350 meters to go. The boat began to move, reeling the leaders in seat by seat. With 300 meters to go, the American boys pulled even with Italy and Germany. Approaching the final 200 meters, the boys pulled ahead by a third of a length.

Bobby Moch glanced up ahead at the huge black-and-white "Ziel" sign—the German word for "Finish." He began to calculate just what he needed out of the boys. He decided it was time to start lying.

Moch barked, "Twenty more strokes!" He started counting them down, "Nineteen, eighteen, seventeen, sixteen, fifteen ... Twenty, nineteen ..." Each time he hit fifteen he reset back to twenty, hoping the boys wouldn't notice. In a daze, the boys threw their long bodies into each stroke, rowing furiously, flaw-lessly, and with uncanny elegance. Their oars were bending like bows, the blades entering and leaving the water cleanly, smoothly, efficiently. The shell ghosted forward between pulls, its sharp cedar prow slicing through the dark water. Boat and boys were forged together, bounding fiercely forward like a living thing now.

They were in full-sprint mode, pulling forty strokes per minute, when they hit a wall of sound. The boat had reached the bleachers on the north side of the course. In lane six, the boys were not more than ten feet away from the edge of the stands. Thousands of spectators stood over them, screaming, "Deutsch-land! Deutsch-land! Deutsch-land!" The sound utterly drowned out Bobby Moch's orders. Not even Don Hume, sitting just eighteen inches in front of Moch, could understand the coxswain.

The Italians surged. So did the Germans. All three leaders were rowing at a full sprint. The race was even again. Moch yelled and screamed, but nobody heard him. Joe didn't know what was happening, except that he hurt like he'd never hurt in a boat before. He felt like hot knives were stabbing the muscles in his arms, legs, and back. Every desperate breath burned his lungs.

On the balcony of Haus West, Hitler dropped his binoculars to his side. He rocked back and forth with the chanting of the crowd. His henchmen, Goebbels and Göring, were cheering wildly. On the balcony next door, Al Ulbrickson stood motionless. His face was blank. He fully expected to see Don Hume collapse over his oar at any moment. Back home in Seattle, the radio announcer was screaming. Harry and Joyce and all the kids couldn't make out what was happening, but they were all on their feet.

Out of the corner of his eye, Moch saw the Germans and Italians surging again and knew that the boys had to go still higher, to give even more than they were giving, even as he knew they were already giving everything they had. With the wooden handles at the ends of his steering lines, he started banging on ironwood knocker boards on the outside of the boat. Even if the boys couldn't hear his commands, maybe they could feel the vibrations, and know he needed more. They did. They understood that it was a signal to do what was impossible, to go even higher. Somewhere deep down inside, each of them grasped at shreds of will and strength they did not even know they possessed.

The gold medal finish, USA in the far lane

The three boats stormed toward the finish line, the lead going back and forth. Hume took the beat higher and higher until the boys hit forty-four. They had never rowed at this rate before. They'd never even thought it was possible. They edged narrowly ahead. The Italians began to close again. The Germans were right beside them. "Deutsch-land! Deutsch-land! Deutsch-land!" thundered in the boys' ears. Bobby Moch was pounding the wood, screaming words no one could hear. The boys took one last mighty stroke and hurled the boat across the line.

On the balcony Hitler raised a clenched fist shoulder high. Goebbels leapt up and down. Hermann Göring slapped his knee, a maniacal grin on his face.

In the American boat, Don Hume bowed his head as if in prayer. The German stroke oar toppled backward into the lap of his number seven man. In the Italian boat, somebody leaned forward and vomited overboard. The crowd continued to roar, "Deutsch-land! Deutsch-land! Deutsch-land!"

Nobody knew who had won.

The American boat drifted on down the lake, beyond the grandstands, into a quieter world. The boys leaned over their oars, gasping for breath, their faces still shattered by pain.

Finally the loudspeakers crackled back to life with the official results. The bow of the American boat had touched the line six-tenths of a second ahead of the Italian boat and exactly a second ahead of the Germans. The chanting of the crowd faded suddenly.

On the balcony of Haus West, Hitler turned and strode back into the building, unspeaking. His henchmen scurried in behind him. The American boys did not understand the announcement at first. But when they did, their grimaces of pain turned suddenly into broad smiles.

In Seattle, Joe's half siblings whooped and hollered and cheered and tumbled about the house. Harry applauded. Joyce cried. With tears streaming down her face, she carefully returned the four-leaf clover to her book and hugged Harry for the first time ever.

The boys rowed slowly past the grandstands to polite applause. Al Ulbrickson and George Pocock shoved their way through the crowds, desperately trying to get to their crew. The boys pulled up to the float in front of Haus West. An official presented them with an enormous laurel wreath. Al Ulbrickson arrived on the float breathless and crouched down by the boat. The wreath had been passed from boy to boy. He pointed to it and grumbled to Roger Morris, "Where'd you get the hay?" Roger motioned over his shoulder with his thumb and said, "Picked it up downstream."

The boys climbed out of the shell and stood at attention while a German band played "The Star-Spangled Banner." Then they shook some hands, hoisted the *Husky Clipper* onto their shoulders, and carried it back to the shell house. In their dirty sweatshirts and mismatched shorts, they looked as if they'd just come in from an ordinary workout on Lake Washington. But as their coach would soon attest, they were no ordinary crew. A reporter stopped Ulbrickson on the way into the shell house and asked him what he thought of his boys. For once, Ulbrickson didn't hesitate before he spoke. "They are," he said, "the finest I've ever seen in a shell."

The next day, the boys prepared the *Husky Clipper* for shipment back to Seattle, put on their Olympic dress uniforms, and headed to the grand Olympic Stadium in Berlin. After the gold medal soccer match between Austria and Italy, the boys took to the field to receive their medals. As they lined up next to the German and

The medal ceremony, Bobby Moch on the podium

Italian crews, Olympic officials went down the American line, hanging gold medals around the boys' necks and placing small laurel wreaths on their heads. Their names appeared on the enormous forty-three-foot-wide announcement board at the eastern end of the stadium. "The Star-Spangled Banner" began to play, and the American flag slowly ascended a flagstaff behind the announcement board. As Joe watched the flag rise with his hand over his heart, he was surprised to find that tears had crept into the corners of his eyes. Moch choked up too. So did Stub McMillin. By the time it was over, they were all fighting back tears.

That night, as the boys went out on the town, Joe stayed in. He lay awake all night. He spent much of the night simply staring at his gold medal where it hung at the end of his bunk. As much as he had wanted it, and as much as he understood what it would mean to everyone back home, he realized that the medal wasn't the most important thing he would take home from Germany.

Immediately after the race, even as he sat gasping for air in the *Husky Clipper*, not sure whether they had won, a sense of calm had enveloped him. In the last desperate sprint to the finish—in the searing pain and bewildering noise of the last few moments—Joe had realized with startling clarity that there was nothing more he could do to win the race. Except for one thing. He had to abandon all doubt. He had no choice but to throw himself into each stroke as if he were throwing himself blindly off a cliff. He had to trust absolutely that the others would be there to save him from catching the whole weight of the boat on his blade. And he had done it, over and over, forty-four times per minute, not just believing but *knowing* that the other boys would be there for him. All of them.

In those final few meters, Joe and the boys had finally forged the prize they had sought all season, the prize Joe had sought nearly all his life. Each had entirely given himself up to being a part of something larger and more powerful and more important than himself.

Now, finally, Joe felt whole. He was ready to go home.

The 1956 reunion row

# Epilogue

**Within days of the closing ceremony** of the 1936 Olympics, the Nazis renewed their persecution of German Jews and others they deemed inferior. The anti-Semitic signs returned to German streets. The brutality and terror intensified. In December, Hermann Göring met privately with a number of German business leaders and said, "We are already at war. All that is lacking is the actual shooting."

The larger world knew little of these war plans. The illusion surrounding the Olympic Games was complete, the deception masterful. Hitler, Goebbels, and the rest had convinced the world that this new Germany was an advanced, civilized culture. But just three years later—by September 1939, the illusion had utterly fallen away. Hitler invaded Poland and the most catastrophic war in world history was under way. In the next five years, it would take the lives of between fifty and sixty million people. So many died that the exact number would never be known.

After the Olympics, the boys took different routes back to Seattle, and except for Bobby Moch, who graduated, the entire crew was back in the boat by October. On April 17, 1937, they again won the national championship in Poughkeepsie, this time by four lengths, setting a new course record. This was the last race for Joe, Shorty, and Roger. In their four years together, they had never once been defeated.

Joe moved in and lived with his father while he finished at the University of Washington. After he and Joyce were married, they bought a house in Lake Forest Park, near Seattle and not far from the finish line of the Washington-California crew races. He and Joyce would live there for the rest of their lives.

Joe and Joyce on their graduation and wedding day

Joe with his young family

Over the years, they raised five children, and Joyce never forgot what Joe had experienced in his early years. She held true to her promise to make sure that he never went through anything like it again.

In 1941, when America joined in the fight against Germany, some of the boys were too tall to serve as soldiers, but they contributed in other ways. Many of them had earned engineering degrees, and they worked for companies essential to the war effort. Joe worked at the Boeing Airplane Company, where he helped design elements of the B-17 bomber. Gordy Adam worked for Boeing too, and Chuck Day served as a naval doctor in the South Pacific. Shorty Hunt worked as a naval engineer.

The boys remained close for the rest of their lives. They met at least once a year, usually twice, for the rest of their lives. Every ten years, they gathered at the University of Washington, pulled the *Husky Clipper* from its rack, and rowed out onto Lake Washington. At their last reunion row, in 1986, they were one man short of a crew, as Chuck Day had died of lung cancer. Their backs were aching, their joints troubled. But they dipped white blades into the water and glided out onto Lake Washington, still pulling together as one. Then, with evening coming on, they hobbled back up the ramp to the shell house, waved to photographers and put their oars in the racks for the last time.

Joe in the woods

In August of 2011, I traveled to Berlin to see where the boys had won gold seventy-five years earlier. I visited the Olympic Stadium and then took the train out to Köpenick, wandering through its cobblestone streets. I walked past the vacant lot where the town's synagogue stood until the night of November 9, 1938, when a torch-bearing mob looted it and burned it to the ground.

In Grünau I found the regatta grounds little changed from 1936. The covered grandstands still rise near the finish line. The Langer See is still placid and tranquil. Young men and women in racing shells still row in racing lanes laid out just as they were in 1936. Late that afternoon, I stood on the balcony of Haus West. I remained there for a long, quiet minute, near where Hitler stood seventy-five years before. Standing there, it occurred to me that when Hitler watched Joe and the boys fight their way back from the rear of the field to sweep ahead of Italy and Germany, he was watching his own doomed future. He did not know that one day hundreds of thousands of boys just like them would return to Germany, dressed in the olive drab uniforms of the American army, intent on hunting him down.

By the time I visited Germany, Joe had passed away. A few years earlier, Joyce had died as she had lived, holding Joe's hand. The rest of the boys were gone as well. But there is one survivor of the 1936 gold medal race: the *Husky Clipper*. She hangs in the light, airy dining room of Washington's Conibear Shellhouse. Suspended from the ceiling, she is a graceful needle of cedar and spruce. Her red and yellow woodwork gleams under small spotlights. Beyond her, on the eastern side of the building, Lake Washington spreads out behind a wall of glass.

Every fall several hundred freshmen—men one day, women another, most of them tall, a few of them noticeably short—assemble beneath her on early October afternoons. They fill out registration cards. They anxiously look around the room. They chat nervously until the freshman coach steps in front of them and calls for quiet in a loud, no-nonsense voice. As they settle down, he begins to

The *Husky Clipper* where it hangs today

talk to them about what they can expect if they seek a spot on his crew. Mostly, at first, he talks about how hard it will be. Then he shifts his tone a bit and begins to talk about the glory of earning a chance to pull one of the white blades of Washington. He talks about recent victories and the now age-old rivalry with California.

Finally he pauses, clears his throat, raises his hand, and points up at the *Husky Clipper*. Several hundred necks crane. The freshmen gaze upward. A new, deeper level of quiet settles over the room. And then he begins to tell the story.

Royal Brougham's Olympic
press badge

# TIMELINE OF EVENTS

**March 1914:** Joe Rantz is born in Spokane, Washington, a former lumber town on the banks of a cold, clear river.

**Spring 1918:** After his mother, Nellie, passes away, Joe lives with various relatives before settling back in with his father, Harry, who has remarried.

**June 28, 1919:** World War 1 ends.

**Summer 1924:** Harry's new wife Thula demands Joe leave the family home. Joe is forced to earn his shelter and meals on his own.

**1925:** Harry and Thula pack up their three kids, retrieve Joe, and move to Sequim, Washington. In Sequim, Joe meets Joyce Simdars.

**October 29, 1929:** The stock market crashes and the United States plunges into the Great Depression.

**November 1929:** Returning from school, Joe finds Harry, Thula, and their kids packed and ready to leave. Once again, Joe is left behind.

**September 1933:** After finishing high school, then working for a year to save money, Joe moves to Seattle and enrolls at the University of Washington.

**October 5, 1933:** Nazi dictator Adolf Hitler inspects the grounds for the new Olympic Stadium to be built outside of Berlin, Germany.

**November 28, 1933:** Following weeks of grueling tryouts, Joe earns a spot on the University of Washington's freshman rowing team.

**April 13, 1934:** The boat's first big race is the Pacific Coast Regatta in Seattle's Lake Washington. With Joyce watching from a ferry full of cheering students, the freshman crew sweep past their archrivals from the University of California.

**June 16, 1934:** The freshman boys win the national championships in Poughkeepsie, New York, by an astonishing five boat lengths.

**Summer 1934:** As much of the country suffers from an intense heat wave, Joe spends the summer in Sequim, working and saving money.

**January 1935:** Head coach Al Ulbrickson announces the team's new goal: to represent the U.S. at the 1936 Olympics in Berlin.

**Spring 1935:** Joe's team once again places first at the Pacific Coast Regatta, but then the coach demotes Joe and his teammates. The new varsity loses to Cal at the national championships.

**April 3, 1935:** Joe surprises his father Harry at work. It's the first time in more than five years he's seen his dad.

**Summer 1935:** Joe gets a job working on the Grand Coulee Dam, a massive construction project. He spends his days hanging from a cliff, pounding at rock walls with a jackhammer.

**September 15, 1935:** In Germany, where preparations for the Games are well underway, Adolf Hitler announces laws that essentially make it illegal to be Jewish. Given these developments, Americans began questioning whether the United States should even send an Olympic team to Berlin.

**October 25, 1935:** Joe learns that Thula has passed away from an infection.

**December 8, 1935:** Despite many protests, including a ten-thousand person anti-Nazi march in New York City, the American Olympic Committee decides against boycotting the games in Berlin. The United States will be going to the Olympics after all.

**March 7, 1936:** Thirty-thousand German troops roll into the Rhineland, a former German territory that was supposed to be a peaceful zone. The takeover is later recognized as one of the first major steps toward World War II.

**April 18, 1936:** In the Pacific Coast Regatta, Joe and his new crew blow California out of the water and smash the course record by an amazing 37 seconds.

**June 22, 1936:** Although Cal had been stroking impressive times in practice, sparking many to wonder if they'll win, the boys from Washington claim a dramatic victory at the national championships in Poughkeepsie.

**July 5, 1936:** At the Olympic Trials in Princeton, New Jersey, Joe and the boys win the right to represent the United States at the 1936 Olympic Games.

**July 24, 1936:** The Washington crew arrives in Germany. All violence and hatred in Berlin has been hidden from public view.

**August 14, 1936:** With Adolf Hitler watching from a balcony, and Joyce and his family listening on the radio back home in Seattle, Joe and the boys surge from dead last all the way to first place, winning the gold medal by a fraction of a second.

# THE ART OF ROWING
## as taught by Al Ulbrickson

In their best moments, the eight boys in the Husky Clipper row as one. Facing the back of the boat, each of the young men sits on a small seat that slides back and forth along greased tracks. They strap their feet into stationary pedals. Each rower grabs hold of his oar, pulls himself into position, and waits for the signal from the race's starter.

Once they begin to row, each boy repeats the following steps over and over. They push through this sequence thirty to forty times per minute, in near-perfect rhythm, until their race is complete.

**1. Ready:** Facing the back of the boat, the oarsman begins in a curled-up position. His chest is bent over his knees. His arms are stretched out in front of him, gripping the oar. The blade of each oar is out of the water.

**2. Catch:** Once the starter gives the signal, each boy drops the blade into the water and leans back hard, toward the bow. His arms remain straight as the blade grabs the water; he lets his back do all the work.

**3. Drive:** As his shoulders pass over the center of his body, he straightens his bent knees, pushing hard with his legs. His seat begins sliding toward the front of the boat. At the same time, he pulls the handle of the oar nearly to his chest.

**4. Layback:** The muscles in his back, arms, legs, and chest all work together to pull the oar and push the blade against the water, driving the boat forward. When each rower's still-straight back is leaning slightly toward the bow, and his legs are extended, he has reached the limit of his stroke.

**5. Release:** All at once, each rower drops his hands toward his waist and pops the blade up out of the water. At the same time, he rolls one wrist, turning the oar so the blade is flat, parallel to the surface.

**6. Recovery:** To prepare for the next stroke, he pushes his arms toward the back of the boat, rotates his shoulders forward, and pulls his knees up toward his chest. As he returns to the crouched position, he rolls his wrist back so the blade is again perpendicular to the surface. He is ready to drop it down and start his catch at the exact same moment as every other boy in the boat.

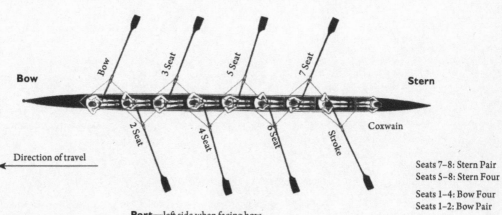

**Starboard**—right side when facing bow

Bow · 3 Seat · 5 Seat · 7 Seat

**Bow**      **Stern**

2 Seat · 4 Seat · 6 Seat · Stroke

Coxwain

Direction of travel

**Port**—left side when facing bow

Seats 7–8: Stern Pair
Seats 5–8: Stern Four

Seats 1–4: Bow Four
Seats 1–2: Bow Pair

Notes and Index TK